Vehicle Safety Inspection Systems

Vehicle Safety Inspection Systems

How Effective?

W. Mark Crain

American Enterprise Institute for Public Policy Research
Washington, D.C.

W. Mark Crain is associate professor of economics at Virginia Poly-
technic Institute and State University and research associate at the
University's Center for Study of Public Choice.

Library of Congress Cataloging in Publication Data

Crain, W. Mark.
    Vehicle safety inspection systems.

    (AEI studies ; 258)
    Includes bibliographical references.
    1. Automobiles—Inspection—United States.   2. Traffic
safety—United States.   I. Title.   II. Series: American Enterprise
Institute for Public Policy Research.   AEI studies ; 258.
TL285.C72   614.8'62   79-26143
ISBN 0-8447-3361-X

AEI studies 258

Printed in the United States of America

CONTENTS

6 REGULATION FOR PUBLIC OR SPECIAL INTEREST   47

7 SUMMARY AND CONCLUSION   64

APPENDIX A: Alternative Specifications of the Empirical Model   66

APPENDIX B: Test for Reverse Causation   69

LIST OF TABLES

ACKNOWLEDGMENTS

I am grateful to James Buchanan, Roger Faith, William A. Jordan, Roland McKean, Gordon Tullock, Richard Wagner, Finis Welch, and Asghar Zardhooki for useful discussions and suggestions at various points during the preparation of the manuscript. The diligent research assistance provided by Barry Baysinger, Henry Butler, Harold Elder, Fred Kuchler, and Matt Smith is also gratefully acknowledged. Especially, I wish to thank Robert Tollison for his unwavering encouragement and constructive criticisms. I am also indebted to James Miller, Marvin Kosters, Brad Behrman, Jeff Eisenach, and others associated with the American Enterprise Institute who gave extensive comments, criticisms, and suggestions for improving the final draft. Finally, I am grateful to Pat Bagby and Judy Wood Baker for their excellent typing and editing of the manuscript, as well as to the editors at AEI, particularly Margaret Seawell and Susan Rideout.

1
Introduction

Vehicle safety inspection requirements constitute one of the lesser known sets of safety regulations issued by the Department of Transportation through its National Highway Traffic Safety Administration (NHTSA). These requirements are important: mandatory inspection programs are now found in over half of the states, and about 76 million vehicles are inspected annually.[1]

The implementation of vehicle inspection systems has been part of a more general effort by the states to develop highway safety programs in accordance with the uniform safety standards promulgated by NHTSA between 1967 and 1972. With reference to the requirements set forth in 23 U.S.C. 402, the secretary of transportation cannot apportion any federal funds for safety programs (averaging about $2.175 million per state in 1977) to any state which has not established a NHTSA-approved program.[2] Although subsequent legislation and court interpretations have not been construed to require the secretary to demand compliance with every single standard issued by NHTSA, adoption of the prescribed regulations, including inspection programs, has been the most common way by which states have qualified under federal-aid agreements.[3]

The federal government's emphasis on state vehicle safety inspection programs has continued unabated despite a lack of any evidence that the programs actually improve highway safety. Indeed, if anything, proponents of vehicle inspection seem to be

---

[1] U.S. National Highway Traffic Safety Administration, *An Evaluation of the Highway Safety Program*, DOT HS-802, July 1977, p. III-5.

[2] U.S. Department of the Treasury, *Federal Aid to States, Fiscal Year 1977*, p. 16.

[3] U.S. National Highway Traffic Safety Administration, *Highway Safety Program Manual*, vol. 102 (February 1978), p. I-3.

increasing pressure and even broadening their horizons. Proposals are being advanced for a national system of vehicle inspection, administered by the federal government.[4] In many of the existing state programs the goals of vehicle inspection have been broadened to include control of auto emissions and increased fuel economy.[5] Since the raison d'être of vehicle inspection was to reduce mechanically caused vehicle accidents and since the experience with inspection for emission and fuel economy purposes is so short, this study will concentrate on the efficacy and efficiency of vehicle inspection in improving highway safety. The analysis, of course, may well be relevant to other related issues.

Deaths, injuries, and destruction of property in accidents are clear and unsettling costs of automobile usage. In 1974, for example, over 46,000 drivers, passengers, and pedestrians were killed, and 1,800,000 persons suffered disabling injuries as a result of vehicle accidents. Estimates of the aggregate social cost of the 1,240,000 highway accidents in 1974 range upward from $19.3 billion.[6] Motor vehicle accidents are, in fact, the leading source of accidental deaths, injuries, and property damage in the United States. It is understandable that policy makers are seeking improvements in highway safety—which is, after all, the announced goal of mandatory vehicle safety inspections.

---

[4] See the *Washington Post*, Sunday, April 17, 1977, p. G8 and the task force report, "How to Save 624,000 Barrels of Crude Oil Daily Through Periodic Motor Vehicle Inspection," presented by the following trade associations: Motor Equipment Manufacturers Association, Automotive Parts Rebuilders Association, Automotive Warehouse Distributors Association, Automotive Parts and Accessories Association, Automotive Service Industry Association, Specialty Equipment Manufacturers Associations, and Automotive Boosters Club International.

[5] NHTSA, *An Evaluation of the Highway Safety Program*, p. III-4. Congressional acts to expand the objectives of inspection programs include the Clean Air Act Amendments of 1970 and 1977 and the Motor Vehicle Information and Cost Saving Act of 1972. Under the Clean Air Act Amendments of 1977 the Environmental Protection Agency must require states in which at least one major metropolitan area fails to meet National Ambient Air Quality Standards for ozone and carbon monoxide by 1982 to establish emissions system inspection and maintenance programs in those metropolitan areas. Based upon State Implementation Plans received from the states during 1979, some twenty-nine states will have to develop and implement such programs. For preliminary evaluations of the effectiveness of inspection programs in the area of controlling automobile emissions, see Paul Downing, "An Economic Analysis of Periodic Vehicle Inspection Programs," *Atmospheric Environment*, vol. 7 (1973), pp. 2137-2146; and Downing and William Watson, Jr., "The Economics of Enforcing Air Pollution Controls," *Journal of Environmental Economics and Management*, vol. 1 (1974), pp. 219-236.

[6] See National Safety Council, *Accidents Facts* (Chicago, 1975) and U.S. National Highway Traffic Safety Administration, *1975 Societal Costs of Motor Vehicle Accidents*, 1976.

The first purpose of this study is to find out whether additional safety is provided by the various types of state inspection programs currently employed under federal mandate. The basic hypothesis of the programs is that, everything else being equal, highway death and accident rates will be detectably lower where mandatory vehicle inspection systems are in force. An investigation of the performance records of existing state programs, however, yields no evidence that vehicle inspection systems are effective in reducing highway deaths or accidents.

In light of a lack of evidence that vehicle inspections are effective, the second purpose of the study is to analyze the basic premises and suppositions underlying inspection policies. For example, since the immediate goal of vehicle inspection is to eliminate mechanical failures, examination of the extent to which mechanical failures cause highway accidents is relevant. Moreover, it seems appropriate to question whether and in what ways vehicle inspection programs do, in fact, reduce defect-caused accidents. Finally, the study examines the economic impact of inspection regulations, making some tentative estimates of economic efficiency and distributional effects.

At this point it should be emphasized that this study is not intended to deny or denigrate the importance of the real costs associated with vehicle accidents. Instead, the point is that vehicle inspection systems have little or no effect on these costs, while imposing sizable direct and indirect costs on millions of vehicle owners.

Chapter 2 of this volume sketches the legislative history of vehicle inspection and describes the legal status of current inspection programs. The reliance on inspection as a method of safety protection is quite old, and its continued existence—indeed its proliferation—shows how a costly regulatory policy can grow in spite of any indication of effectiveness. Chapter 3 looks at the stated purpose of the federal standard for vehicle inspection and examines the premises upon which that standard is based. Chapter 4 examines empirical relationships between alternative systems of vehicle inspection and highway safety (measured in several ways). As a number of recent studies point out, the efficacy of regulatory activity cannot be resolved on the basis of theory alone. Evaluation of government policies must ultimately rest on empirical evidence.[7]

---

[7] For examples, see Sam Peltzman, "An Evaluation of Consumer Protection Legislation: The 1962 Drug Amendments," *Journal of Political Economy*, vol. 81, (September/October 1973), pp. 1049-1091; Sam Peltzman, *Regulation of Auto-*

In view of a lack of evidence that vehicle inspection is effective, Chapter 5 reexamines the premises underlying the whole program. Analytical models are employed to predict the nature of inspection services under various regulatory regimes as a means of understanding the disparity between the goals of inspection laws and their actual accomplishments. Chapter 6 considers reasons for the persistence and proliferation of mandatory vehicle inspection requirements, drawing on recent contributions to the economic theory of regulation. In addition to looking at potential private-sector beneficiaries, there is a discussion of the financing, licensing, and procedural aspects of inspection systems. Finally, Chapter 7 summarizes the study's findings and outlines the implications for public policy.

---

mobile Safety (Washington, D.C.: American Enterprise Institute, 1975); Robert S. Smith, *The Occupational Safety and Health Act: Its Goals and Achievements* (Washington, D.C.: American Enterprise Institute, 1976); and Lester B. Lave and Warren E. Weber, "A Benefit-Cost Analysis of Auto Safety Features," *Applied Economics*, vol. 2 (1970), pp. 265-275.

2

Legislative History and Legal Status of Vehicle Inspection Regulation

State vehicle inspections designed to improve highway safety were begun in Massachusetts in 1926. Compliance was actively encouraged but was made voluntary. The following year, as part of their "save-a-life" campaigns, the governors of New York and Maryland similarly appealed to drivers to obtain vehicle checkups at officially designated service stations. By 1929, the legislatures in Pennsylvania, Maryland, Delaware, and New Jersey had enacted laws requiring periodic vehicle inspections at officially licensed garages and service stations. In 1946, with twelve other states having enacted similar laws, the President called a highway safety conference whose deliberations reflected the increasingly popular view that maintenance and repairs should be encouraged or perhaps mandated by the states. In fact, the conference recommended that states pass laws requiring periodic vehicle inspection.

For the next twenty years the adoption of laws to require vehicle inspection was left entirely to the discretion of individual state and local governments, and by 1966, twenty-one states had passed laws of this sort. In that year Congress enacted two laws now generally regarded as the foundation of current automobile safety regulation and vehicle inspection systems. These were the Highway Safety Act (23 U.S.C. 401 et seq.) and the National Traffic and Motor Vehicle Safety Act (15 U.S.C. 1381 et seq.).

The 1966 Statutes

The federal laws directed the secretary of commerce (with authority subsequently transferred to the secretary of transportation) to conduct research on traffic accidents causing death and injury, to develop uniform safety standards, to see that the states adopted them, and to provide financial assistance for state programs designed to promote effective motor vehicle safety standards.[1] The Highway Safety Act of 1966 (Section 402) specifically stated that the uniform safety standards to be issued by the secretary should include provisions for vehicle registration, operation and inspection.

In 1967, the Department of Transportation (DOT) began issuing its initial standards for highway safety programs. By 1972, eighteen standards had been issued—of which the very first dealt with periodic motor vehicle inspection (which, to avoid the overuse of acronyms, hereafter is called simply vehicle inspection). The possibilities of vehicle inspections were initially investigated by the department's highway safety arm, the National Highway Traffic Safety Administration, with the help of states that had previously adopted inspection programs and of groups such as the American Association of Motor Vehicle Administrators, the National Committee on Uniform Traffic Laws and Ordinances, and the International Association of Chiefs of Police.[2]

Concepts emerging from NHTSA's investigation were the idea that periodic inspection should be a required part of each state's highway safety program and the view that federal funds should be provided to assist the states in carrying out such programs. In line with this, the initial standard issued by NHTSA in June 1967 provided that

> each state shall have a program for periodic inspection of all registered vehicles or other experimental, pilot, or demonstration program approved by the secretary, to reduce the number of vehicles with existing or potential conditions which cause or contribute to accidents or increase the severity of accidents which do occur, and shall require the owner to correct such conditions.[3]

In addition, NHTSA established the following qualifications defining what constituted inspection within the meaning of the standard:

> A. Every vehicle registered in the State is inspected at the time of initial registration and at least annually thereafter, or at such other times as may be designated under an experimental, pilot or demonstration program approved by the secretary.

---

[1] The responsibilities and authority assigned to the secretary of transportation which deal explicitly with the development of state highway safety programs are contained in Section 1392 of the National Traffic and Motor Vehicle Safety Act of 1966 and Sections 401, 402, and 403 of the Highway Safety Act of 1966.

[2] NHTSA, *An Evaluation of the Highway Safety Program*, p. III-3.

[3] NHTSA, *An Evaluation of the Highway Safety Program*, p. 24.

B. The inspection is performed by competent personnel specifically trained to perform their duties and certified by the state.

C. The inspection covers systems, subsystems, and components having substantial relation to safe vehicle performance.

D. The inspection procedures equal or exceed criteria issued or endorsed by the National Highway Safety Bureau.[4]

This initial standard thus dealt principally with the scope and frequency of vehicle safety inspections and not directly with their quality nor with specific procedures to be used in finding vehicle defects. Neither did it specify criteria for rejecting inspected cars, although the Highway Safety Act of 1966 required that these criteria be issued by September 1968. From the time NHTSA issued this initial standard in 1967 to the present, ten additional states adopted vehicle inspection programs and five states dropped their inspection requirements, bringing the total number of state programs in compliance with this standard to twenty-six.

Each state had until December 31, 1969, to carry out plans that met the eighteen federal standards issued by NHTSA or to show reasonable progress toward this goal; otherwise, federal highway safety funds could be denied. The law, however, did permit a temporary waiver of any standard (for up to three years) if a state was carrying out a substitute program approved by NHTSA.[5] The temporary waiver was designed to allow adequate time for the states and NHTSA to evaluate the safety quality of experimental or substitute plans. After the three-year waiver, a state could apply to NHTSA to substitute the state's pilot plan as a permanent part of its overall highway safety program.

The Highway Safety Act of 1966 authorized the secretary of transportation to see that states established the uniform standards issued by DOT or approved substitutes as part of their state highway safety programs and supplied several means of assuring compliance.[6]

---

[4] Ibid.

[5] The criteria used by NHTSA for approving an experimental program as a justification for waiving periodic inspection require that it must (1) demonstrate a positive safety effort on the entire experimental sample of vehicles; (2) provide reasonable assurance that, if implemented statewide, it could provide adequate coverage to the state's total vehicle population; (3) exhibit results equal to or superior in safety quality to those which could be achieved under a periodic motor vehicle inspection program. See, U.S. General Accounting Office (GAO), *Report to the Congress: Effectiveness of Vehicle Safety Inspections Neither Proven Nor Unproven*, December 20, 1977, p. 7.

[6] These sanctioning and incentive provisions are contained in Section 402 of the Highway Safety Act of 1966.

First, the secretary was ordered not to release any safety program funds appropriated by Congress to any state that did not have an approved safety program. Second, he was authorized to cut a state's portion of federal highway construction funds by 10 percent. And third, additional "incentive" grants were authorized for those states having made the most significant progress toward carrying out approved safety programs and toward reducing traffic fatalities. (These incentive grants were not to exceed 25 percent of a state's portion of federal highway safety funds—amounting in the aggregate to nearly $120 million in fiscal year 1977.)[7] In effect, the freedom of the states to decide for themselves whether or not to adopt vehicle inspection systems was being restricted, though not, of course, entirely overriden.

The first showdown over state compliance came in 1970 when DOT threatened to authorize reductions in federal funds to non-complying states. For two reasons, this threat was not carried out. First, NHTSA decided to accept "spot" or random inspections as a temporary substitute for periodic inspections (albeit somewhat reluctantly) if the state had a good reason for postponing adoption of a "full inspection plan." Second, Congress, under pressure from representatives in the noncomplying states, decided that to withhold highway funds from states that did not have periodic inspection programs would make driving particularly dangerous in those states (reasoning that states without inspections would need *better* roads than other states to offset the lack of inspections). Without full congressional support for required periodic inspection, DOT in effect adopted the position (1) that the financial burden of inspection could only be justified where there were corresponding safety benefits, and (2) that the information gathered to that point did not support the imposition of an elaborate periodic inspection scheme.[8] This weakened position was reflected in NHTSA's reluctance to issue the anticipated detailed quality specifications—vehicle-in-use standards (VIU)—which specify exactly what parts of the vehicle should be checked and the methods of inspection.

Vehicle-In-Use Standards and Inspection Quality

NHTSA found itself in an awkward position. On the one hand, the National Traffic and Motor Vehicle Safety Act of 1966 required issuance of VIU standards by September 1968, and on the other,

---

[7] U.S. Department of the Treasury, *Federal Aid to States, Fiscal Year 1977*, p. 15.
[8] "Where is PMVI Today?" *Jobber and Warehouse Executive*, January 1974.

NHTSA lacked adequate evidence of the need to develop specific details for a national periodic inspection standard. By August 1971, NHTSA had finally organized a research program designed to gain the information necessary for VIU standards and to convince states of the merits of these standards. The task force conducting this research recommended in November 1971 that NHTSA should *not* issue VIU standards until its preliminary procedures had been thoroughly validated. The plan issued by NHTSA in April 1972 had the following goals:

> 1. to establish safety performance criteria for motor vehicle operations and recommended inspection procedures by June 1973, with emphasis on brakes, steering, suspension, and tires; and
> 2. to develop a prototype inspection program by June 1973 as a means of encouraging states to use the recommended criteria and procedures and for proving that motor vehicle inspection systems can reduce accidents and a proportional number of injuries and fatalities with a favorable cost-benefit ratio.[9]

NHTSA was clearly taking a cautious position toward the development and issuance of VIU standards to guide state vehicle inspection programs. This, at least implicitly, seemed to reflect NHTSA's awareness that without evidence of the effectiveness of such programs in reducing accidents, the standards should not be issued. (And, of course, without this evidence, the states would be more reluctant to comply with the standards.)

Congressional and Court Pressure

NHTSA's strategy of proceeding with research and development before issuing VIU standards was short-lived, however. Congress—and more specifically the Senate Commerce Committee—interpreted NHTSA's position as foot-dragging, and in July 1972 reprimanded NHTSA (and the Department of Transportation generally) for its failure to meet the September 1968 deadline for VIU standards.[10] Pressure to comply with the congressional mandate for vehicle-in-use standards peaked on July 21, 1973, when the U.S. District Court of the District of Columbia ordered the secretary of transportation

---

[9] GAO, *Report to the Congress*, p. 7. The prototype inspection program was never carried out, probably because (as discussed in the text) NHTSA issued the vehicle-in-use standards in 1973, before the results of the prototype program could have been used for this purpose.

[10] GAO, *Report to the Congress*, p. 7.

to publish VIU standards for vehicles weighing 10,000 pounds or less by September 1973 and VIU standards for vehicles weighing over 10,000 pounds by August 1974.[11] Thus, even though NHTSA had not planned to issue the specific VIU regulations for state inspection programs until the relevant research data had been evaluated, these standards were issued (as ordered) in September 1973. For vehicles weighing 10,000 pounds or less, the standards covered the vehicle's brake system, brake power unit, steering unit, suspension system, tires, and wheel assemblies. For vehicles over 10,000 pounds, the standard covered, in addition, the more sophisticated brake systems used on such heavier vehicles.

In approving federal funding of state highway safety programs, NHTSA assigned a high priority to implementation of these VIU standards for vehicle inspection. This move was made largely because of the ruling by the U.S. District Court, but it created a wave of resistance to the VIU standards, even in those states which had previously adopted less stringent vehicle inspection programs. The new standards were considerably more stringent than the old and hence more costly to motorists, and, even more important perhaps, there was little evidence that they improved vehicle safety. In an attempt to pacify the motorists in those states affected (that is, in the states which had programs that did not cover the VIU standards), NHTSA allowed the states until June 30, 1978, to comply with all periodic inspection standards, including those for vehicles in use. States were required, however, to demonstrate some progress toward full integration of the VIU standard into their safety programs by June 30, 1976, or risk reductions in federal funds.[12] This deadline was subsequently moved to the end of the 1978 fiscal year, September 30, 1978.

Rather than adopting the federal periodic inspection plan and VIU standards, thirteen states by 1975 had chosen temporary experimental programs and had these approved by NHTSA (as permitted by the legislation) in order to avoid federal sanctions. Four of these states—Michigan, California, Connecticut, and Ohio—adopted random, or spot check, vehicle inspection procedures. These temporary experimental programs have since expired in California and Ohio, and NHTSA did not approve their requests for a permanent substitution of random inspections for the federally outlined program of periodic inspection of each vehicle. Failure to approve came

---

[11] Ibid., and Rommel Consultants, *State of Alaska: Periodic Motor Vehicle Inspection Survey and Plan* (Ingram, Texas: November 1, 1974), appendix 10.
[12] GAO, *Report to the Congress*, p. 7.

because in NHTSA's opinion these states had not shown that random inspection was as effective as periodic inspection and because NHTSA was not convinced that checks provided adequate coverage of all vehicles in the state (which may amount to much the same thing).[13] The status of the remaining eleven states that chose substitute or experimental programs in place of inspection and vehicle-in-use standards is uncertain, since only one of these states (as of the beginning of 1979) has formally requested NHTSA to approve their pilot program as a permanent substitute for periodic inspection.

Perhaps as the result of pressure from some members of Congress and from certain consumer groups, NHTSA began late in 1976 sanctioning procedures directed at noncompliance with federal standards for state highway safety programs. The particular standard at issue dealt with motorcycle helmet safety, and sanctions were directed at three states, California, Illinois, and Utah.[14] Once again, NHTSA's attempt to enforce state compliance with its guidelines was derailed by Congress. With a strong negative reaction to the sanctions from the noncomplying states, Congress passed legislation that temporarily removed NHTSA's sanctioning authority. The Highway Safety Act of 1976 (P.L. 94-280, 90 Stat. 451) stated that until June 29, 1978, NHTSA could not withhold federal funding for the highway safety programs or reduce the allocations of federal funds for highway construction for failure of any state to adopt an approved highway safety program.[15] Moreover, the act required NHTSA to present to Congress by July 1, 1977, an evaluation of each of the Highway Safety Program Standards issued since 1967.[16]

Current Status of Vehicle Inspection

In its July 1977 report to Congress, NHTSA offered the following assessments of the eighteen highway safety program standards in general and of vehicle inspection programs in particular.

> The report's principal recommendation is that the Federal insistence on mandatory compliance with each of the present 18 Highway Safety Program Standards be replaced with a more flexible stance. That, in the future, greater reliance must be placed upon State and local highway safety

---

[13] Ibid., p. 8.

[14] Ibid., p. 9.

[15] Ibid., p. 11.

[16] NHTSA, *An Evaluation of the Highway Safety Program*. The congressional mandate for the evaluation is in Section 208(b) of the 1976 Highway Safety Act.

agencies to identify their most pressing problems and advance appropriate solutions to them.

. . . based on many years experience, it was evident that the evaluation of standards would not lead to the discovery of any clear linkage between any specific standard and changes in the number of accidents, injuries, or fatalities on a national level.[17]

In essence, NHTSA's recommendation to Congress was that failure to comply with the federal vehicle inspection standard should not result in disapproval of a state's highway safety program and, hence, the withholding of federal funds.

On the basis of somewhat erratic behavior of Congress toward vehicle inspection over the past twelve years, it is difficult to predict how and whether Congress will react to NHTSA's recent recommendation. It is important to note in this regard that in response to this policy position taken by DOT, the General Accounting Office recommended on December 20, 1977, that Congress "reject the [Transportation] Department's recommendation which would make compliance with the Federal vehicle inspection standards optional"[18] and argued that "the potential contribution of safety inspections for improving highway safety is too great to deemphasize the standard as a completely optional program requirement, as proposed by DOT."[19]

The final legislative action that has been taken by the U.S. Congress which is relevant to state safety programs was the Highway Safety Act of 1978 (P.L. 95-599). Section 207 of this act amended only slightly the original content of the Highway Safety Act of 1966, stating explicitly that the secretary of transportation was authorized to waive standards on a temporary basis, where new or experimental programs were implemented, "including, but not limited to, such programs for identifying accident causes, adopting measures to reduce accidents, and evaluating the effectiveness of such measures." This small amendment, however, is quite important in practice. In effect, although the requirement for inspection systems remains intact, the annual approval of state safety programs has become more of a discretionary action by NHTSA. Based on its 1977 evaluation of the standards, NHTSA does not appear to

---

[17] NHTSA, *An Evaluation of the Highway Safety Program*, preface.

[18] GAO, *Report to the Congress*, p. i.

[19] Ibid., p. 13. The positions taken by GAO reflect, to a large extent, the proposals offered by the National Conference of Governors' Highway Representatives to NHTSA.

TABLE 1

State Vehicle Inspection Programs

State	Present Law Enacted	Program Started	Administered by	Inspections per Year[b]
Arkansas	1967	1969	State Police	1
Colorado	1935	1936	Revenue Department	2
Delaware[a]	1933	1933	Division of Motor Vehicles	1
District of Columbia[a]	1938	1939	Division of Motor Vehicles	1
Florida	1967	1968	Highway Patrol	1
Georgia	1963	1965	Public Safety	1
Hawaii		1961	County Police	1 or 2
Idaho[c]	1967	1968	Law Enforcement Department	1
Indiana	1967	1969	Traffic Safety & Vehicle Inspection Department	1
Iowa	1974	1975	State Department of Transportation	1
Kentucky[c]	1966	1968	State Department of Transportation; Bureau of Vehicle Registration	1
Louisiana	1960	1961	Public Safety	1
Maine	1930	1930	State Police	2
Massachusetts	1926	1930	Division of Motor Vehicles	2
Mississippi	1960	1961	Public Safety (Vehicle Inspection Department)	1
Missouri	1967	1969	Highway Patrol	1
Nebraska	1967	1969	Division of Motor Vehicles	1
New Hampshire	1930	1931	Division of Motor Vehicles	2
New Jersey[a]	1936	1938	Division of Motor Vehicles	1
New Mexico[c]	1937	1959	Division of Motor Vehicles	2
New York	1954	1957	Division of Motor Vehicles	1
North Carolina	1965	1966	Division of Motor Vehicles	1
Oklahoma	1967	1969	Public Safety	1
Pennsylvania	1927	1929	State Department of Transportation	2
Rhode Island	1958	1959	Division of Motor Vehicles	1
South Carolina	1967	1968	Highway Department	1
South Dakota[c]	1967	1968	Highway Patrol	1
Texas	1951	1951	Public Safety	1

(Table continued on next page)

13

TABLE 1 (continued)

State	Present Law Enacted	Program Started	Administered by	Inspections per Year[b]
Utah	1936	1936	Division of Motor Vehicles	1
Vermont	1935	1936	Division of Motor Vehicles	2
Virginia	1932	1932	State Police	2
West Virginia	1953	1955	Public Safety	1
Wyoming[c]	1967	1967	Revenue Department	1

[a] State-operated stations; in states not so indicated, stations are state-appointed and supervised.

[b] Most states with year round inspection designate which month vehicle is to be inspected, according to date of purchase, license tag digits, or the like. Some states, as indicated, limit inspections to certain periods of the year.

[c] Laws requiring inspection programs have been repealed subsequently.

SOURCE: Highway Users Federation for Safety and Mobility and American Association of Motor Vehicle Administrators.

be inclined to reject state programs which do not include mandatory inspection plans. This current practice by NHTSA has restored somewhat the freedom for the individual states to tailor programs to their particular needs and makes even more relevant the question of the merits of periodic inspection programs.

As of July 1979, thirty-two states and the District of Columbia had enacted some form of regulatory provisions attempting to improve highway safety through mandatory vehicle inspection systems, although five of these states (Idaho, Wyoming, New Mexico, Kentucky, and South Dakota) have subsequently repealed their laws. Table 1 summarizes the current state programs. Two of the states having inspection programs (Kansas and Wyoming) are still administering temporary experimental programs approved by NHTSA, and twenty-three states have no program currently in operation. As of 1979, only three states (Virginia, New Hampshire, and Pennsylvania) had fully complied with the VIU standards issued in September 1973, and seven states (Colorado, Georgia, Missouri, New York, Rhode Island, Utah, and West Virginia) had partially complied by meeting the VIU standard for wheel removal to check a vehicle's braking system.

3

Vehicle Inspection: Purpose and Premises

The purpose of periodic motor vehicle inspection, as it was initially stated by the National Highway Traffic Safety Administration is "to increase . . . the likelihood that every vehicle operating on the public highways is properly equipped and is being maintained in a reasonably safe working condition."[1] The basic premises underlying vehicle inspection are, first, that mechanical defects or equipment failures are a significant source of highway accidents and, second, that periodic inspection can detect, identify, and rectify these defects and prevent these failures—thus reducing the number and severity of motor vehicle accidents.[2] Public opinion surveys indicate that vehicle operators even in states without mandatory inspection requirements tend to accept these premises and generally support some form of mandatory inspection though there is no consensus on the exact inspection procedures.[3]

Given the number of individuals affected by vehicle inspection programs (about 76 million vehicles were inspected in 1976) and the resources consumed, it is odd that few rigorous attempts have been made to evaluate the effectiveness of these programs.[4] Moreover, if vehicle inspection programs do indeed reduce accidents, a

---

[1] NHTSA, *An Evaluation of the Highway Safety Program*, p. III-3.

[2] U.S. National Highway Traffic Safety Administration, *Costs and Benefits of Motor Vehicle Inspections*, January 1975, p. 7.

[3] There does appear to be more disagreement over the manner in which mandatory inspections should be performed than over their general efficacy. See Harold W. Sherman, *Sampling of Driver Opinions Toward Periodic Motor Vehicle Inspection* (Ann Arbor: University of Michigan Highway Safety Research Institute, 1969), especially p. 41; and Jay S. Creswell, Jr., "Driver Characteristics Affecting Vehicle Condition and Response to a Motor Vehicle Inspection Program," *HIT Lab Reports*, vol. 4, no. 6 (February 1974).

[4] NHTSA, *An Evaluation of the Highway Safety Program*, p. III-5.

means for reducing the substantial costs to society of highway accidents (by a Department of Transportation estimate over $20 billion in 1975) may have been underutilized.[5]

As Chapter 1 has indicated, the Department of Transportation was pressured by Congress and at one point ordered by the U.S. District Court to issue specific inspection regulations. The pressure for NHTSA to evaluate the effectiveness of periodic inspection has been no less intense, although NHTSA has attempted to maintain a more flexible position. In lieu of conclusive research efforts, NHTSA has simply had to assume that vehicle inspection reduces accidents in order to make its benefit-cost calculations appear reasonable. For example, NHTSA has estimated that vehicle inspection would have to eliminate 14 to 39 percent of the highway accidents caused by mechanical defects in order for it to be cost-effective.[6] The assumption that the actual effectiveness of periodic inspection in reducing accidents is within this 14 to 39 percent range is (as NHTSA points out) based on spotty and certainly nondefinitive data gathered primarily by three states (Alabama, Nebraska, and Texas) on their own respective state programs.[7] For roughly fifty years, vehicle inspections have been made without real evidence that this measure is effective in reducing accidents.[8]

Before looking at the evidence brought together in the present study, the basic premises underlying the argument for vehicle inspection should be examined.

Vehicular Defects and Accidents

The first question to be considered is the extent to which mechanical failures contribute to motor vehicle accidents. On this matter, some evidence is available. Several studies indicate that only about 6 percent of highway accidents may be definitely attributed to mechan-

---

[5] NHTSA, *Costs and Benefits of Motor Vehicle Inspections*, p. 7.

[6] Ibid., p. 29.

[7] Ibid., p. 9.

[8] Several empirical studies have been performed but none has provided conclusive findings. Particularly, none definitely supports the hypothesis that mandatory periodic inspections reduce accident rates. See Robert C. Buxbaum and Theodore Colton, "Relationship of Motor Vehicle Inspection to Accident Mortality," *Journal of the American Medical Association*, vol. 197, no. 1 (July 4, 1966), pp. 101-106; Victor R. Fuchs and Irving Levenson, "Motor Accident Mortality and Compulsory Inspection of Vehicles," *Journal of the American Medical Association*, vol. 201, no. 9 (August 28, 1967), pp. 87-91; NHTSA, *Costs and Benefits of Motor Vehicle Inspections*, p. 5; and School of Urban and Public Affairs, *An Assessment of Pennsylvania's Periodic Motor Vehicle Inspection System* (Pittsburgh: Carnegie-Mellon University, December 1975).

ical failure.[9] In view of the costs, it is not obvious, therefore, that attempts to reduce accident rates through improving the way vehicles function mechanically will be cost-effective. To put it another way, resources devoted to producing highway safety by vehicle inspection designed to reduce mechanical failures may not necessarily have a very high return relative to other ways of improving motor vehicle safety (higher liquor taxes or more driver education programs, for example).

Behavior of Vehicle Operators

The second question to be considered is whether purely voluntary behavior leads to an underinvestment in vehicle safety maintenance —or, to put it less technically, if cars are not inspected periodically, will they be properly maintained? Clearly, mandatory inspection implies that the answer to this question is "no." Since the goal of periodic inspection is to ensure that only mechanically safe vehicles are on the road, the suggestion is that without mandatory inspections drivers would not choose to invest sufficiently in safety maintenance. This would occur only if drivers do not internalize all the relevant (expected) costs of an accident; that is, the driver believes he will not have to pay all the costs. Whether this assumption is reasonable, however, cannot be determined on purely theoretical grounds, since it cannot be known, a priori, if all the (expected) costs of accidents are borne by the parties responsible. If there are external (spillover) costs from vehicle accidents (that is, costs to individuals who are not at fault), then a case might be made for governmental intervention. But whether such intervention is warranted depends on the extent of such spillovers and the cost of remedying this market imperfection through government action. In other words, are the imperfections created by regulation greater than or less than the market imperfections it seeks to address?

A second question is whether individual drivers use safer driving techniques (for example, slower speeds or less tailgating) if their cars are less than safe mechanically. This is essentially the point raised by Sam Peltzman in his investigation of the effects of requir-

---

9 For examples, see Indiana University Institute for Research in Public Safety, *Tri-Level Study of the Causes of Traffic Accidents* (prepared for the U.S. Department of Transportation, National Highway Traffic Safety Administration under NHTSA Contract No. DOT-HS-034-3-535, January 1975); NHTSA, *Costs and Benefits of Motor Vehicle Inspections,* p. 8; and James M. Compton, Gerald S. Griffith, and W. R. Hansley, *The Pennsylvania Periodic Motor Vehicle Program* (Skippensbury State College, July 1975).

ing seat belts and air bags. Peltzman argues that it "is not that the required safety devices have failed to do their intended work. They *do* work, but their very efficacy has created forces that in fact have compromised their lifesaving potential." [10] If a reduction in the likelihood of injury in an accident gives rise to less careful driver behavior with more risk-taking (less safe driving habits, as Peltzman's evidence suggests), then an increased likelihood of injury, resulting from improper maintenance, would normally lead to safer driving in other respects.

The fact that individuals will adjust their driving behavior simply reflects the broader phenomenon that everyone chooses safety in varying degrees and accomplishes it in varying ways. For example, differences may be observed in the speeds people drive, in the amount of intoxicants they consume before (or while) driving, in their obedience to traffic signals, and in their clearance distances when passing. These decisions all reflect differences in individual preferences for safety—as does the extent to which individuals maintain the mechanical condition of their vehicles. Maintenance, however, is only one factor involved in highway safety, and even if it is capable of being carried out by regulation, drivers will still choose an overall level of risk-taking that satisfies their individual safety standards. Adjustments in driver behavior—which alter the effectiveness of safety regulations generally—are a complicating factor in determining the value of mandatory inspection programs.

Feasibility of Anticipating Mechanical Failures

Even if it is assumed that purely voluntary behavior produces a "sub-optimal" amount of safety, it must still be determined whether a vehicle inspection requirement improves matters. That is, will mechanical defects be detected, will equipment failures be anticipated, and will the appropriate corrective measures be taken to rectify unsafe conditions? Can defects in mechanical equipment such as brake linings develop during the interval between the required inspections and hence go unnoticed if inspections are periodic? To be sure, if all potential sources of mechanical failure were replaced at periodic inspection intervals, the likelihood of accidents might be reduced, but this might well constitute an overinvestment in vehicle safety.[11]

---

[10] Peltzman, *Regulation of Automobile Safety*, p. 1.

[11] Moreover, there is already a potential bias toward overinvestment in mechanical maintenance where repair stations do the inspecting (for reasons discerned later).

And there is one more question to be raised here. If it is agreed that mechanical failures cause accidents, that all costs are not internalized without government intervention, and that anticipating mechanical failure is technically feasible, are there appropriate incentives for the inspectors to do their jobs? That too is a matter for empirical investigation.

Summary of Unresolved Issues

In summary, the present federal government position of regulating automobile safety by mandatory periodic inspections has evolved over the last fifty years, and most drivers are inclined to believe that vehicle inspections improve highway safety. But there are several important questions that have not been subjected to careful empirical investigation.

(1) Even if vehicle inspection in and of itself improves safety, its effect may be dissipated if drivers take more risks than they would if cars were not periodically inspected or if they assume (perhaps erroneously) that periodic inspection will take care of mechanical defects.

(2) Even if voluntary behavior produced suboptimal investment in vehicle maintenance, and hence in highway safety, it is not obvious, a priori, that vehicle inspections are a feasible means of detecting equipment problems.

(3) Even if it is technically feasible to detect mechanical problems, it is not clear that inspection agents have sufficient incentives to perform well in their jobs.

(4) Even if vehicle inspection does lead to corrections in mechanical problems, the programs may not be a cost-effective means of improving highway safety.

(5) The extent to which individuals know and take account of the expected costs of highway accidents is not known, a priori. Hence, it is not clear that drivers underinvest in vehicle safety maintenance in the absence of periodic inspection requirements.

4

The Effects of Vehicle Inspection

Two basic questions pertaining to vehicle inspection programs are examined in this chapter: (1) are these programs effective in reducing highway accidents? and (2) are some types of vehicle inspection systems more effective than others? Since different inspection procedures are employed in different states, and some states have no inspection requirements at all (see Table 2), comparative data for a given year can be used to estimate relationships between inspection procedures (or the lack thereof) and highway safety.

Of course, highway safety records (the dependent variable) are a function of many factors. The equations presented here incorporate the following independent variables: (1) the existence and nature of inspection systems, (2) population density, (3) median family income, (4) fuel consumption, (5) federal highways, (6) population age, (7) procedure for driver's license renewal, (8) alcohol consumption, and (9) minimum damage required for reporting an accident. In short, differences in safety records among states are "explained" by these nine variables, in order to isolate the effect of state inspection systems, the focus of this study.

In these equations, three different measures of state accident rates are used:[1]

(1) death rate (number of highway safety deaths per year per registered vehicle),

---

[1] It should be pointed out that, of these three measures of accident rates, the death rate is the most reliable since accidents not involving a fatality are more likely to go unreported and hence unrecorded in the highway statistics. Data sources are: for the death rate, National Safety Council (NSC), *Accident Facts* (Chicago: NSC, 1975); and for the nonfatal injury rate and the nonfatal accident rate, U.S. Federal Highway Administration, *Fatal and Injury Rates on Federal-Aid and Other Highway Systems*, 1975.

TABLE 2

Inspection Procedures among the Various States

State	Annual Periodic Inspections	Biannual Periodic Inspections	Spot Inspections	State Owned and Operated Inspections	No Inspection Requirement
Alabama	X[a]				
Alaska			X		
Arizona					X
Arkansas	X				
California			X		
Colorado	X				
Connecticut			X		
Delaware	X			X	
Florida	X				
Georgia	X				
Hawaii	X				
Idaho	X[b]				
Illinois					X
Indiana	X				
Iowa			X[a]		
Kansas					X
Kentucky	X[b]				
Louisiana	X				
Maine		X			
Maryland					X[c]
Massachusetts		X			
Michigan			X		
Minnesota			X[a]		
Mississippi	X				
Missouri	X				
Montana	X				
Nebraska	X				
Nevada					X
New Hampshire		X			
New Jersey	X			X	
New Mexico		X[b]			
New York	X				
North Carolina	X				
North Dakota					X
Ohio			X		

(Table continued on next page)

TABLE 2 (continued)

State	Annual Periodic Inspections	Biannual Periodic Inspections	Spot Inspections	State Owned and Operated Inspections	No Inspection Requirement
Oklahoma	X				
Oregon			X		
Pennsylvania		X			
Rhode Island	X				
South Carolina	X				
South Dakota	X[b]				
Tennessee	X[a]				
Texas	X				
Utah	X				
Vermont		X			
Virginia		X			
Washington			X		
West Virginia	X				
Wisconsin			X		
Wyoming	X[b]				

[a] Localities within the state may require periodic inspections.
[b] Inspection program dropped since 1976.
[c] Only required for purposes of titling used vehicles.
SOURCE: Council of State Governments, *Book of the States* (Lexington, Kentucky: Iron Works Pike, 1976).

(2) nonfatal injury rate (number of individuals injured per year per 1,000 vehicle miles), and

(3) nonfatal accident rate (number of nonfatal accidents per year per 1,000 vehicle miles).

Outlined below are the reasons the nine independent or "explanatory" variables were selected and the hypothesized effect of each one.

(1) *Inspection system.* State inspection systems can be classified in several ways for purposes of statistical analysis. As will become clear, five basic definitions were used, each designed to evaluate the effect of a particular type or aspect of an inspection program. The presumption to be tested is that, everything else equal, accident rates will be lower where vehicle inspection is present than where it is not.

(2) *Population density.* This variable, defined as state population per square mile of land area, is included for two reasons: (1) to some extent it measures differences in urban and rural driving conditions, reflecting the degree of traffic congestion, and (2) to some extent it reflects differences in vehicle speeds (lower in the city than in the country). More densely populated states could be expected to have higher accident rates overall because of traffic congestion, but lower fatal accident rates because of lower average vehicle speeds.[2]

(3) *Fuel consumption.* Per capita fuel consumption is intended to measure the degree of driving intensity. Higher per capita fuel consumption will generally reflect more motor vehicle activity in a state and, hence, can be expected to increase vehicle accident rates.[3]

(4) *Median income.* Median family income is included for two reasons. First, driving is likely to be a "normal" good—that is, more driving is "consumed" as income increases, so that higher income levels should be associated with more driving and, hence, with higher accident rates. Second, however, income is also related to education level, which in turn should be related to the skill of drivers in judging and observing traffic laws. In sum, while those with higher incomes may drive more and, therefore, tend to be involved in more accidents, these accidents are likely to be less severe. Income should be positively related to nonfatal accident rates, but negatively related to highway death rates.[4]

(5) *Federal highways.* This is the proportion of road mileage within the state constructed with federal aid. It is included to represent differences in the quality of roads in different states, assuming that the federal interstate highway system is of better quality than state roads. The expected effect of highway quality on accident rates is uncertain because, on the one hand, better quality roads (that is, more interstate highways) can be expected to reduce the likelihood of accidents, but on the other hand, these roads will also increase average vehicle speed (which increases the likelihood and severity of accidents). Thus, the expected net impact of this variable is indeterminate.[5]

(6) *Population age.* This variable is defined as the percentage of the state's population between eighteen and twenty-four years

---

[2] Data source for population density: U.S. Bureau of the Census, *U.S. Census of Population: 1970*, vol. 1, part A.

[3] Data source for fuel consumption: U.S. Federal Highway Administration (FHA), *Highway Statistics*, 1975.

[4] Data source for median income: U.S. Department of Commerce, *Statistical Abstract of the United States*, 1975.

[5] Data source for federal highways: FHA, *Highway Statistics*.

of age. The relationship between population age and accident rate is indeterminate on a priori grounds—which may seem at first to run against conventional wisdom.[6] While the accident rate among young drivers is higher than for the population as a whole, it does not necessarily follow that the percentage of population between eighteen and twenty-four will have a positive effect on accident rates. While young drivers have higher probabilities of being involved in accidents, both the expected costs of their accidents and therefore their insurance rates are likewise higher than average Hence, the number of young drivers is predictably lower than would be the case in the absence of insurance requirements, which means simply that the percentage of young citizens in the population at large may not accurately reflect the percentage of young drivers in the state—data for which is not directly available. The net effect of population age is therefore unclear, contrary to the expectations (but not the findings) of earlier studies.[7]

(7) *License renewal.* Following the procedure developed in a previous empirical investigation of state inspections, this is entered into the regression equation as a dummy variable, equal to *one* if an eye test and a written test are required for license renewal and *zero* otherwise.[8] The relationship between strictness of license renewal and accident rates should be negative, if the stricter procedures are effective in screening drivers.

(8) *Alcohol consumption.* Driving while intoxicated is a strong contributing factor to highway accident rates. The extent of drinking and driving has not been measured directly, although several previous studies have used per capita consumption of alcohol as a proxy. A positive relationship between alcohol consumption and accident rates would be expected.[9]

(9) *Reporting requirements.* This variable is included only in the equations which involve nonfatal accident rates. It is entered into

---

[6] For an example, see Fuchs and Levenson, "Motor Accident Mortality."

[7] Data source for population age: Department of Commerce, *Statistical Abstract of the United States, 1975.*

[8] Data source for license renewal: American Automobile Association (AAA), *Digest of Motor Laws* (Falls Church, Virginia: AAA, 1976). The specification for this variable follows the procedure used by Fuchs and Levenson, "Motor Accident Mortality."

[9] Data source for alcohol consumption: Favin-Jobon Company, *The Liquor Handbook* (New York, 1974). Previous studies which have used per capita alcohol consumption as a measure of driving under intoxicating influences include Peltzman, *Regulation of Automobile Safety;* Fuchs and Levenson, "Motor Accident Mortality"; and School of Urban and Public Affairs, *An Assessment of Pennsylvania's Periodic Motor Vehicle Inspection System.*

the equations as a dummy variable with one of three values: *minus one* if accidents with less than $100 damage must be reported, *zero* if the minimum is $100 to $200, and *plus one* if the minimum is $200 to $400. Higher reporting minimums suggest that fewer accidents will be reported, and fewer accidents reported will lower nonfatal accident rates (fatal accidents will have to be reported in any case).[10]

Data used for all nine independent variables are from the year 1974, the most recent year for which all data are available. The continuous (nondummy) variables—that is, accident rates (all three measures), population density, fuel consumption, median income, federal highways, population age, and alcohol consumption—are entered in the form of logarithmic transformation which compares percentage changes, rather than absolute numbers.[11] The estimated coefficients of the variables in the equations can thus be interpreted as the percentage change in an accident rate that is likely to result from a given percentage change in each of the independent variables (or, in the economist's term, as elasticities).[12]

The equations presented here are only a small sample of those that were examined during the course of this study; however, they are the ones that seem to work best. Appendix A contains a brief discussion of other equations that were tried and their effects on the findings.

The first set of equations discussed here compares accident rates in states with periodic vehicle inspection programs to accident rates in states having either a random inspection program or no program at all. The second comparison includes states where cities require vehicle inspections but no statewide program exists. The third comparison is between those states requiring twice-yearly periodic inspections and all the rest. The fourth compares states providing inspections through publicly owned facilities with those that do not. The fifth focuses on those states employing random or spot-check inspection procedures as opposed to periodic inspection and noninspection states. In each set of equations, the particular inspection system under review is demarcated from those of the remaining states by a

---

[10] Data source for reporting requirements: AAA, *Digest of Motor Laws.*

[11] See Fuchs and Levenson, "Motor Accident Mortality," for a previous example of a logarithmic specification of the regression model.

[12] I can report that the results of regressions estimated using the linear values of the variables were not substantially different from those presented in the text. The overall "fit" or explanatory power of the equations was, in general, better using the logarithmic transformations.

dummy variable (assigned a value of *one* in each state using the particular system and *zero* for the remaining states).[13]

Periodic Inspection Systems

The first (and most important) empirical question is whether the existence of vehicle inspection is statistically and significantly related to highway accident rates. The inspection system (dummy) variable is defined as *one* for all states employing some form of statewide periodic inspection (yearly or twice-yearly) and *zero* otherwise. For expository convenience, this definition of the inspection system dummy variable and the set of equations using it is denoted as "Model A." The second definition of the inspection system dummy variable sets the variable equal to *one* for those states which have either statewide or some locally required system of periodic inspection, and equal to *zero* otherwise. This is "Model B."

In both Models A and B the inspection system dummy variable should show a significant negative relationship to accidents (however measured) if periodic inspection requirements are effective in reducing accident rates. That is, everything else equal, in states having vehicle inspection programs accident rates will be lower than average, and in states not having such programs accident rates will be higher than average. A positive or insignificant relationship would suggest that the inspection programs are not effective.

The results from Models A and B using 1974 data are presented in Table 3. T-ratios (that is, statistical measures of significance) are listed in parentheses. The present study is primarily interested in the signs and significance of the coefficients for the inspection system variables. One useful way of judging the particular model is to look at how much of the state variations in accident rates it explains—information provided by the R^2 statistic. The R^2 statistic in the first column of Table 3 indicates that the regression model "explains" (or accounts for) about 76 percent of the variation in death rates across states. By the standards for this kind of analysis, the overall explanatory power of the regression equation is quite good. Likewise, in the remaining models, the regression equations "explain" about three-fourths of the variations in death rates (Tables 3 through 6).

---

[13] If there are systematic differences in accident rates between those states with the specified inspection system and those without, these differences will be detected (and measured) by the dummy variable. The estimated coefficient for the dummy variable will measure the effect of the given inspection system on highway accident rates. Data source for inspection system: Council of State Governments, *Book of the States, 1974-1975* (Lexington, Kentucky: Iron Works Pike, 1975), p. 365.

TABLE 3

Statewide and Locally Required Periodic Inspections

Independent Variables	Model A Dependent Variables			Model B Dependent Variables		
	Death rate	Nonfatal injury rate	Nonfatal accident rate	Death rate	Nonfatal injury rate	Nonfatal accident rate
Constant	−0.77	−1.70	−2.83	−1.68	−0.16	−1.55
	(−0.32)	(−0.49)	(−0.85)	(−0.69)	(−0.04)	(−0.44)
Periodic inspections	0.11	0.04	0.02	0.15	−0.06	−0.06
	(1.73)	(0.47)	(0.21)	(2.01)	(−0.51)	(−0.58)
Population density	−0.17	0.09	0.10	−0.17	0.11	0.11
	(−5.30)	(2.00)	(2.17)	(−5.43)	(2.28)	(2.41)
Fuel consumption	0.08	−0.08	−0.09	0.08	−0.11	−0.11
	(1.76)	(−1.33)	(−1.44)	(1.82)	(−1.66)	(−1.72)
Median income	−0.72	1.34	1.36	−0.62	1.20	1.24
	(−3.66)	(4.64)	(4.89)	(−2.94)	(3.82)	(4.13)
Federal highways	0.01	0.06	0.04	0.02	0.05	0.04

(Table continued on next page)

TABLE 3 (continued)

Independent Variables	Model A — Death rate	Model A — Nonfatal injury rate	Model A — Nonfatal accident rate	Model B — Death rate	Model B — Nonfatal injury rate	Model B — Nonfatal accident rate
	(0.88)	(2.25)	(1.88)	(1.03)	(2.18)	(1.82)
Population age	−0.31 (−0.63)	−1.62 (−2.24)	−1.40 (−2.02)	−0.31 (−0.63)	−1.59 (−2.20)	−1.39 (−2.00)
License renewal	−0.07 (−1.15)	0.15 (1.68)	0.16 (1.86)	−0.08 (−1.35)	0.18 (1.91)	0.17 (2.05)
Alcohol consumption	0.10 (1.07)	−0.17 (−1.32)	−0.16 (−1.31)	0.10 (1.03)	−0.18 (−1.35)	−0.17 (−1.33)
Reporting minimum	—	−0.002 (−0.03)	0.01 (0.11)	—	−0.01 (−0.15)	−0.001 (−0.01)
R^2 (coefficient)	0.7584	0.5377	0.5738	0.7639	0.5382	0.5770
$F_{(9,40)}$	16.09	5.17	5.99	16.58	5.18	6.06
N observed	50	50	50	50	50	50

The other regression equations consistently "explain" about 50 to 60 percent of the variations in nonfatal accident and nonfatal injury rates across states (see Tables 3 through 6)—also an acceptable level for analysis of this type. The F-statistics (provided for each of the regression results in Tables 3 through 6) provide a direct test for the overall explanatory power for the regressions. The values of the respective F-statistics indicate a 99.5 probability that the explanatory variables have an effect on the accident rate variables and that the results are not just a fluke. Put another way, there is only one-half of 1 percent probability that the regression results occur simply by chance.

The inspection system variables in Models A and B test the hypothesis that mandatory periodic inspections improve highway safety by reducing accident rates. None of the six estimated relationships presented in Table 3 offers evidence to support this hypothesis. In fact, the sign of the inspection variable in the death rate regressions is positive—meaning that higher than expected death rates are associated with the existence of inspection programs. However, all the relationships between periodic inspection and nonfatal injury and accident rates are statistically insignificant. This means there are no detectable (nonrandom) differences in nonfatal accident or injury rates between those states with periodic inspection programs and those without—which may be directly interpreted as meaning that nonfatal injury and accident rates have not been reduced by periodic inspection requirements. Perhaps more startling is the appearance of positive relationships between the periodic inspection variables and death rates. In Model A the relationship is significant at the 90 percent level and in Model B at the 95 percent level. A full discussion and interpretation of this finding will be provided in Chapter 5, but clearly vehicle inspection programs do not have the expected effect of reducing accident rates.

The findings that mandatory inspections do not reduce injury and nonfatal accident rates and that death rates are systematically higher in states with requirements might be challenged in line with the following reasoning. States experiencing relatively high fatality/ accident rates may tend to institute inspection requirements, while states with lower rates may not. If high-rate states adopt mandatory inspection, they may actually have decreased their accident rates without bringing them down to levels in noninspecting states with fewer accidents. In such circumstances, the regression analyses here may fail to identify the true effects of mandatory inspection.

One way of dealing with the "reverse causation" question is to determine if differences in accident rates existed prior to the issuance of the Federal Standard for safety inspections between states with and without these laws in 1974. Thus a cross-sectional model for 1965 was developed to determine if differences in accident rates existed prior to the issuance of the NHTSA standards for vehicle inspection. If such differences in accident rates are not observed, or if the magnitude of such differences did not diminish between 1965 and 1974, this supports the hypothesis that mandatory vehicle inspection laws have not produced lower accident rates. Alternatively, if differences in accident rates existed prior to 1965, and states complying with NHTSA inspection regulations had comparatively higher accident rates in 1965 than they did in 1974, then this must be interpreted and related to the results for 1974 to see if inspection laws lead to a reduction, even though the complying states still did not have lower accident rates than noncomplying states in 1974. The estimation procedure and the results of this test are provided in detail in Appendix B. Summarizing the relevant findings here, it appears that reverse causation is not a problem with interpreting the 1974 results. We do not find that there was a systematic tendency for higher accident rate states to adopt specific inspection procedures. Moreover, since all states faced the threat of potential financial sanctions by NHTSA (regardless of the level of accident rates), there was a uniform incentive across all the states in 1974 to adopt periodic inspection requirements.

The other variables included in the regression equation for the most part have effects consistent with preliminary expectations. Population density shows a positive and significant relationship with nonfatal accident and injury rates and a negative and significant relationship with death rates—that is, more congested urban areas have more frequent, though less severe, accidents. Fuel consumption, which is the proxy for the intensity of driving activity, is positively related to death rates and negatively related to nonfatal injury and accident rates (which is consistent with the hypothesis that higher driving speeds tend to increase the severity of accidents but not necessarily their frequency), although the levels of statistical significance are more tentative. Median income is negatively related to death rates and positively related to the two measures of nonfatal accident rates (consistent with the hypothesis that if driving increases with income, accidents in higher income states should be more frequent, but that higher incomes are likely to be associated with better driver skills, which should tend to reduce the severity of the accidents). This variable is highly significant throughout. The expected effect of the extent of federal highways was unsure, a priori, since that variable was intended as a measure of road quality (reducing accidents) and of expected driving speed (increasing severity). The net effect appears to be positive in Table 3, but the estimated coefficient, as might be expected, is not consistently significantly different from zero. The coefficients for population age are also not consistently significantly different from zero, but the signs of the coefficients are negative which, as noted, is plausible on a priori grounds. The higher costs of driving activity for young people, resulting from higher insurance rates, suggests a smaller amount of driving activity for this portion of the population, which is precisely what the results in Table 3 suggest. This variable appears at statistically significant levels only in the nonfatal accident regressions.

The Table 3 findings on the importance of alcohol consumption are somewhat mixed and generally not significant. A positive effect of increased per capita alcohol consumption on death rates is suggested for Models A and B, while the opposite effect is suggested on the nonfatal accident measures. Per capita alcohol consumption may not actually be an appropriate proxy for the extent of driving under its intoxicating influence, and it is noteworthy, in this connection, that at least two previous empirical studies were unable to find the predicted effect using this variable as a proxy for drunk driving.[14] Finally, the minimum damage for required reporting of accidents shows no significant relationship to nonfatal accident and injury rates (though the estimated sign is generally negative as expected).

Frequency of Inspection

The second set of estimating equations is designed to examine the relationship (if any) between inspection frequency and accident rates. "Model C" thus defines the inspection system variable as equal to *one* in states employing twice-yearly inspection procedures and equal to *zero* otherwise. The sign of this coefficient should be negative if accident rates are lowered by more frequent vehicle inspections. The results, using 1974 data, are presented in Table 4 (with T-ratios again listed in parentheses). The R^2 (explanatory) values for the three re-

---

[14] Fuchs and Levenson, "Motor Accident Mortality" and School of Urban and Public Affairs, *An Assessment of Pennsylvania's Periodic Motor Vehicle Inspection System* were unable to find the expected statistical relationship for this variable. However, Peltzman, *Regulation of Automobile Safety*, did obtain the expected result using aggregate U.S. data in a time series analysis.

TABLE 4
Twice-Yearly Inspections

Independent Variables	Model C Dependent Variables		
	Death rate	Nonfatal injury rate	Nonfatal accident rate
Constant	0.68	−1.19	−2.68
	(0.30)	(−0.36)	(−0.86)
Biannual inspection	0.03	0.03	0.04
	(0.36)	(0.26)	(0.33)
Population density	−0.15	0.10	0.10
	(−4.86)	(2.17)	(2.27)
Fuel consumption	0.05	−0.09	−0.10
	(1.26)	(−1.52)	(−1.56)
Median income	−0.86	1.29	1.34
	(−4.68)	(4.87)	(5.28)
Federal highways	0.01	0.05	0.04
	(−0.78)	(2.22)	(1.86)
Population age	−0.25	−1.59	−1.39
	(−0.49)	(−2.19)	(−1.99)
License renewal	−0.05	0.17	0.17
	(−0.73)	(1.86)	(1.99)
Alcohol consumption	0.08	−0.18	−0.17
	(0.91)	(−1.36)	(−1.35)
Reporting minimum	—	0.01	0.01
		(0.08)	(0.08)
R^2	0.7415	0.5360	0.5745
$F (9,40)$	14.70	5.13	6.00
N observed	50	50	50

gressions estimated for Model C suggest that 50 to 80 percent of the variations in accident rates are being explained. But the fact that the three estimated coefficients for the twice-yearly inspection variable are not statistically significant suggests that more frequent inspections do not tend to reduce accident rates. None of three measures of highway accident rates appears to be systematically lower in states with twice-yearly inspection. The results for each of the remaining explanatory variables in Model C quite closely resemble the results for these variables in Models A and B.

State Owned and Operated Inspection Systems

The third question with respect to periodic inspection programs is the way in which the inspection service is provided. Specifically, some states designate private service stations to perform inspections, while other states have government owned and operated inspection facilities. (See Table 2.) "Model D" defines the inspection system variable as equal to *one* for states in which the periodic inspection facilities are state owned and operated and *zero* otherwise.

The results from Model D are presented in Table 5. The overall regression equations have roughly the same degree of explanatory power as the equations presented in Tables 3 and 4. The estimated coefficients for the inspection system dummy variable presented in Table 5 do not suggest that accident rates in states where periodic inspections are provided in state-owned facilities are different from accident rates in other states. In none of the three regression equations is this coefficient statistically significant. In other words, the results in this case indicate that having the inspections performed by state-owned stations tends to have no effect on reducing accident rates. The results for the other explanatory variables estimated for Model D are virtually identical to those for Models A, B, and C.

Spot-Check Inspection Systems

The final empirical question addressed in this chapter is the effectiveness of spot-check or random vehicle inspection programs in reducing accident rates. Ten states (see Table 2) received NHTSA approval to use (and in 1974 had implemented) spot-check safety inspections as a temporary substitute for periodic inspections. For at least two of these states (California and Ohio) NHTSA did not approve the random inspection programs as a permanent substitute for periodic inspection, essentially because no evidence was provided on the effectiveness of random inspection programs.[15] An empirical evaluation of their effectiveness is quite relevant because all states must submit their entire highway safety programs to NHTSA for annual approval, and spot inspections are one alternative that many states have turned to.

To examine the impact of spot-check inspection programs on highway safety the inspection system variable is defined as equal to *one* in states which employ spot-checks and *zero* otherwise. This is denoted as "Model E." If the coefficient for the inspection dummy

15 GAO, *Report to the Congress*, p. 8.

TABLE 5

State-Owned Inspection Provision

Independent Variables	Model D Dependent Variables		
	Death rate	Nonfatal injury rate	Nonfatal accident rate
Constant	0.67	−1.96	−2.51
	(0.30)	(−0.33)	(−0.81)
State owned	0.21	−0.06	−0.10
	(1.43)	(−0.27)	(−0.50)
Population density	−0.16	0.10	0.10
	(−5.13)	(2.24)	(2.39)
Fuel consumption	0.06	−0.10	−0.10
	(1.50)	(−1.59)	(−1.68)
Median income	−0.91	1.29	1.36
	(−4.98)	(4.85)	(5.30)
Federal highways	0.02	0.05	0.04
	(0.96)	(2.20)	(1.82)
Population age	−0.15	−1.63	−1.45
	(−0.29)	(−2.23)	(−2.07)
License renewal	−0.04	0.16	0.17
	(−0.66)	(1.81)	(1.92)
Alcohol consumption	0.10	−0.18	−0.17
	(1.09)	(−1.36)	(−1.36)
Reporting minimum	—	−0.004	0.01
		(−0.06)	(0.11)
R^2	0.7530	0.5361	0.5760
$F_{(9,40)}$	15.62	5.14	6.04
N observed	50	50	50

variable in Model E is negative, random inspections would seem to reduce accident rates, while a positive coefficient would suggest the reverse.

The results of the estimations for Model E are presented in Table 6. The findings in this case suggest that spot-check systems tend to reduce highway death rates. The estimated coefficient has a negative sign, consistent with the hypothesis being tested at the statistical significance level of 10 percent. In other words, there is a 90 percent probability that death rates will be lower in states using random inspection than in other states (including those states having periodic inspection programs).

TABLE 6

Spot-Check Inspections

Independent Variables	Model E Dependent Variables		
	Death rate	Nonfatal injury rate	Nonfatal accident rate
Constant	−0.59 (−0.24)	−2.94 (−0.84)	−4.28 (−1.27)
Spot inspections	−0.10 (−1.32)	−0.14 (−1.27)	−0.13 (−1.23)
Population density	−0.16 (−5.09)	0.09 (2.04)	0.09 (2.15)
Fuel consumption	0.06 (1.48)	−0.08 (−1.32)	−0.08 (−1.37)
Median income	−0.72 (−3.38)	1.48 (4.90)	1.52 (5.22)
Federal highways	0.02 (0.88)	0.06 (2.34)	0.05 (1.97)
Population age	−0.29 (−0.58)	−1.64 (−1.30)	−1.43 (−2.09)
Alcohol consumption	0.07 (0.71)	−0.20 (−1.58)	−0.19 (−1.55)
License renewal	−0.05 (−0.80)	0.16 (1.85)	0.17 (1.97)
Reporting minimum	—	−0.003 (−0.05)	0.01 (0.11)
R^2	0.7512	0.5532	0.5888
F (9,40)	15.48	5.50	6.36
N observed	50	50	50

The estimated relationships between spot inspection and the two measures of nonfatal accident rates are also negative, though less significant (statistically significant only at the 0.15 level).

Finally, Model E "explains" roughly 75 percent of the variation in death rates and 55 to 58 percent of the variations in nonfatal accident rates (see the R^2 statistics in Table 6). Results for the other independent variables are quite similar to the results displayed in Tables 3 through 5.

Summary of the Findings

This chapter has presented an empirical approach to explaining differences in state highway accident and death rates. The regression equations included nine basic independent variables, chosen to explain variations in three measures of highway safety. Overall, the basic equation "explains" from 50 to 80 percent of the differences in accident rates among the states, using 1974 data.

The effects of four specific aspects of state inspection systems were examined within this general estimation procedure. The principal findings may be summarized as follows.

1. When other factors are taken into account, states which employ mandatory periodic inspection programs do not have lower accident rates than those states without such requirements. Thus, periodic inspections do not appear to reduce accidents.

2. Twice-yearly inspections do not appear to be any more effective than yearly inspections in reducing highway accidents.

3. State ownership and operation of periodic inspection stations does not appear to be more effective than appointing private inspection agents or than having no inspection program at all.

4. Spot or random inspection systems appear to exhibit a negative influence on death rates and on nonfatal accident rates, though these results are not entirely conclusive.

5. Relationships between the other explanatory variables and highway accident rates are generally as expected (if not always significant) and appear to be stable and consistent for all definitions of the inspection system variable.

5

Why Have Vehicle Inspection Systems Failed?

The findings presented in the previous chapter suggest that, when other factors are taken into consideration, highway safety in states not using periodic inspections is at least comparable to and perhaps even greater than safety in states where periodic inspection is required. The question is, Why?

Two possible interpretations may be offered. First, any additional resources devoted to vehicle maintenance as a result of periodic inspection simply do not improve the inherent safety characteristics of the vehicle; thus, those expenditures are not effective in reducing accidents. Second, additional expenditures induced by periodic inspections requirements do make the vehicle safer, but this potential for improved highway safety is dissipated by adjustments in driver behavior, as some studies have previously suggested.[1]

Ineffectiveness of Inspections

The first interpretation is supported by four types of additional evidence.

1. Sources of Highway Accidents. As was mentioned in Chapter 1, only a relatively small portion of highway accidents—some 2 to 6 percent—are conclusively attributable to mechanical defects. Table 7 shows the probable sources of highway accidents, according to a recent study conducted for NHTSA by the Institute for Research in Public Safety at Indiana University.

---

[1] Peltzman, *Regulation of Automobile Safety;* and Gordon Tullock, "The Social Costs of Reducing Social Cost," in G. Hasdin and J. Braden, eds., *Managing the Commons* (San Francisco: Freeman and Company, 1977).

TABLE 7
Causal Factors in Motor Vehicle Accidents

Factor	Level of Investigation[a]	Percent of Investigated Cases in Which Factor was Causal[b]	Percent of Cases in Which Factor Increased Accident Severity[b]
Human error	1	83.2	0.5
	2	76.2	0.6
Human condition	1	2.3	0
	2	3.9	0
Environmental	1	16.4	9.0
	2	23.3	3.3
Vehicular condition	1	4.2	0.5
	2	5.7	1.2

[a] Level 1: On-site investigation of accidents immediately following their occurrence by teams of experts.

Level 2: Independent, in-depth investigation of a subset of the accidents investigated on-site, by a multidisciplinary team.

[b] Percentages reflect cases in which there is claim that no doubt exists as to the factors' role and are considered analogous to a 95 percent confidence level.

Source: Indiana University Institute for Research in Public Safety, *Tri-Level Study of the Causes of Traffic Accidents*, National Highway Traffic Safety Administration, Contract Number DOT-45-034-3-535, January 1975.

While it is often quite difficult to determine the causes of vehicle accidents, this study is widely regarded as the best effort to date. It is apparent from Table 7 that human factors (such as excessive speed) are far more important causes of highway accidents than vehicle condition. A significant further reduction in the already small percentage of accidents caused by mechanical failure may simply require more investment in vehicular maintenance than would be induced by existing periodic inspection requirements. Even if more investment were to make a difference, it is not certain how much more would be necessary. The finding in Chapter 4 that twice-yearly periodic inspections do not generate a detectable impact certainly suggests that increasing the frequency of periodic inspections is not the way to achieve additional investment in maintenance sufficient to reduce accidents.

2. Randomness of Equipment Causes of Accidents. Table 8 provides additional findings from the Indiana study mentioned above, breaking

TABLE 8
Equipment Causes of Motor Vehicle Accidents

Cause	Level of Investigation[a]	Percent of Accident Causes[b]	Percent of Increased Accident Severity[b]
Gross brake failure	1	1.4	0.5
(front and/or rear)	2	1.8	0.1
Tire underinflation	1	0	0
	2	0.2	0.1
Tire inadequate tread depth	1	0	0.5
	2	0.7	0.4
Brake imbalance	1	1.4	0
(pulled left or right)	2	0.1	0
Excessive steering freeplay	1	0.5	0
	2	0.1	0.4
Vehicle lights and signals	1	0	0
	2	0.6	0

[a] See Table 7, note a.
[b] See Table 7, note b.
Source: Institute for Research in Public Safety, *Tri-Level Study*.

down the "equipment causes" factor category. It suggests that no single type of vehicular failure causes more than 1.8 percent of highway accidents. This 1.8 percent seems very close to a random effect that may reasonably be expected to occur even with periodic inspection. The fact that no single mechanically related causal factor stands out means that the diagnostic attention or effort of inspectors cannot be concentrated on particular problem areas.

3. Voluntary Incentives. As noted in Chapter 2, there is no clear a priori reason to suppose that individual vehicle operators do not have appropriate incentives for maintaining their vehicles in reasonably good mechanical condition. While it might be plausible in theory to assume that all the costs of undermaintenance may not be borne by the responsible parties (others may be involved in resulting accidents), a counter-argument can surely be made that most of the costs of maintenance (such as correcting the failure of the car to run) are borne by the owners. The finding that only a small percentage of accidents are caused by mechanical defects is consistent with this latter argument. Moreover, there is additional evidence that supports the adequacy of voluntary maintenance incentives: the mean ("normal") time until repairs are made for many "safety sensitive" components is low, while for less safety sensitive parts it is higher. For example, the mean time from detection to repair for brake lights (a safety sensitive component) is 2.8 months, which means that for these types of equipment failures, yearly or even twice-yearly inspections are largely superfluous.[2]

The lack of any safety effect for inspections may therefore stem from the tendency of vehicle owners to repair safety sensitive components such as brakes or lights rather quickly—for obvious reasons. Inspections would therefore be unlikely to intercept those defects which are relatively important in relation to accidents, while detecting such defects as license plate lamps or exhaust systems which rarely cause accidents.

4. Reliability of Inspections. Table 9 offers a final type of evidence for the undetectable marginal impact of additional resources devoted to vehicle maintenance as a result of mandatory inspection requirements. This table deals with the reliability of inspection systems.

This evidence comes from an experiment in which thirteen defects were intentionally created in a 1969 Chevrolet Bel-Air before inspection in Pennsylvania in order to evaluate the detection rate of known defects, as well as the detection rate of nonexistent defects.[3] The highest detection rate of real defects was 54 percent and the rate averaged about 37 percent. Moreover, while the inspection agents sampled in the experiment found on average only about five of the thirteen implanted defects, they "found" on the average two nonexistent defects. If the sample is representative, detection of faulty equipment or mechanical outages by periodic inspection procedures appears to be unreliable. This is not to say that the mechanical condition of vehicles is never improved by inspections; there is, in fact, some evidence that in certain locations inspections do provide such

[2] See James O'Day and Jay S. Creswell, "An Analytical Model of Periodic Motor Vehicle Inspection" (unpublished manuscript, Highway Safety Research Institute, University of Michigan, November 1969); and R. W. McCutcheon and H. W. Sherman, "The Influence of Periodic Motor Vehicle Inspection on Mechanical Condition," *Journal of Safety Research*, vol. 1, no. 4 (December 1969).

[3] School of Urban and Public Affairs, *An Assessment of Pennsylvania's Periodic Motor Vehicle Inspection System*, chapter 2.

It might be noted that this propensity to detect "defects" not present and to overlook true defects is observed in the ordinary auto repair market. See, for example, NHTSA, *Auto Repair and Maintenance: Program to Reduce Consumer Loss*, DOT HS-803-355, May 1978.

TABLE 9
Experimental Findings on Inspection Reliability

Type of Inspecting Agent	Average Number of Real Defects Found as Percentage of Total Implanted Defects[a]	Average Number of Nonexistent Defects Found[b]
Service station	25	1.6
Repair garages	32	1.5
Chain stores	54	1.0
New car dealers	36	3.5

[a] In each trial of the experiment there were thirteen defects implanted in a 1969 Chevrolet Bel-Air.

[b] Nonexistent defects are either (1) nonfaulty parts which the inspection mechanic claimed to be faulty or (2) faulty items which should not be grounds for rejection because they are not included in inspection requirements.

Source: School of Urban and Public Affairs, *An Assessment of Pennsylvania's Periodic Motor Vehicle Inspection System* (Pittsburgh: Carnegie-Mellon University, December 1975), pp. 9-16.

improvement.[4] The point is that inspections appear to be subject to considerable variation, which means that their reliability cannot in general be taken for granted. The incentive structure facing inspection agents—a factor obviously critical to performance and service reliability—will be discussed shortly.

Adjustments in Driver Behavior

A second general explanation for the fact that vehicle inspection programs appear not to reduce accident rates is that adjustments in driver behavior may dissipate the effectiveness of the inspections. This inference is supported by the fact that highway death rates appear to be systematically higher in states with vehicle inspection programs. Two types of adjustments in driver behavior seem plausible in this setting. The first (described by Peltzman) is that safer cars lead to more risk-taking on the part of their drivers.[5] A second behavior adjustment is a perception on the part of drivers that government responsibility for safety maintenance is substituted for individual

---

[4] In fairness, there is evidence that in particular locations periodic inspections do tend to improve the mechanical condition of the vehicles inspected. For example, see McCutcheon and Sherman, "The Influence of Periodic Motor Vehicle Inspection," pp. 184-193. The point I wish to stress is simply that performance of inspections appears to be generally subject to variation.

[5] Peltzman, *Regulation of Automobile Safety*.

responsibility, and thus drivers are lulled into thinking their cars are safer and need less maintenance attention. This possibility is supported by public opinion surveys, which suggest that drivers tend to believe that the mechanical safety of their vehicles is improved by mandatory periodic inspection.[6] Moreover, voluntary safety checks or repairs may simply be postponed until the expiration date of a current inspection certificate, since drivers must bear the inspection costs at that time regardless of mechanical condition.[7] Such behavioral adjustments, if they take place, might account for the higher vehicle death rates in states requiring periodic inspection. In the cases investigated by Peltzman, safety devices were effective, and offsetting behavioral adjustments left highway death rates unchanged; however, if drivers believe that periodic inspection programs improve mechanical safety, but in fact they do not, the net effect could be to increase accident rates.

Incentives and Performance of Private Inspection Agents

With the exception of Delaware, New Jersey, and the District of Columbia, all the states with periodic inspection requirements appoint and license private service stations and garages to perform the inspections. An evaluation of the incentive structure facing these private inspection agents may thus be important in understanding why periodic inspection is not an effective means of reducing accidents. A reasonable assumption is that the objective of private inspection agents is to maximize profits. Normally, this objective would create an incentive for suppliers to provide service of a quality demanded by consumers, and in an important sense the same mechanism that allows consumer preferences to influence the nature of outputs in voluntary exchanges may still be present under the constraints imposed by mandatory periodic inspections. Thus, for example, owners who are coerced into getting their vehicles inspected may seek out those inspection stations which tend to ignore borderline defects as grounds for failing a vehicle—or, for that matter, stations which may be bribed. If the fee for inspection is high, so that the inspecting business is itself profitable, inspection stations will have an incentive to "go easy" on the cars they inspect.

On the other hand, in another (and equally important) sense, consumer sovereignty may be severely impaired by mandatory peri-

---

[6] Sherman, "Sampling of Driver Opinions."

[7] Drivers need not always wait until the expiration date to renew inspections, but to have inspections done earlier means all future inspections of a given vehicle must also be done earlier—which provides an incentive for not going early.

odic inspection. Since owners are required to bear the "fixed costs" of having their cars inspected and since inspection agents are authorized to fail the vehicles they inspect, consumers may be coerced into purchasing parts and service they would not demand otherwise. Thus, if inspection fees are low, and there is no bribery, service stations that are also vehicle inspection stations may require unnecessary repairs in order to make money.

Minimizing the Inspection Hassle. Involuntary consumption of periodic inspections, by the very nature of coercive transactions, is likely to create an incentive (at least among some vehicle owners) to minimize the price of obtaining certification. Since the monetary fee that inspection stations may charge is fixed and uniform for all relevant competitors (that is, within the geographic boundaries of the state or locality), competition among inspection stations then could take the form of reducing other costs of inspections—for example, time cost or the extent of repairs required before approval is granted. However, one ramification of this form of nonprice competition is that the probability of detection of mechanical defects is lower in this "minimum hassle" type of service. Similarly, owners of inspection stations are not likely to hire highly skilled, highly paid mechanics to perform inspections for consumers who prefer "minimum hassle" service. Such cost reductions and specialization in making inspections could, therefore, be a means for station owners to increase their profits. For the individual station owner, behavior would hinge on the answer to the question, "Is there more to be made by making inspections or by making repairs?" The extent of substandard inspections is likely to increase with less careful monitoring of the performance of inspection and with lower penalties for improper inspection performance. Since only about half of the states having vehicle inspection programs monitor the performance of their inspection facilities, there would appear to be substantial room for operators specializing in "minimum hassle" service. Penalties for improper inspection performance range from warnings and temporary suspension of inspection certificates to revocation of certificates, fines, and jail terms. Such actions against inspection stations are usually begun, however, in response to consumer complaints.[8] The effectiveness of these sanctions on inspection performance is dubious since consumers who patronize "minimum hassle" stations are not likely to complain.

---

[8] See American Association of Motor Vehicle Administrators, *Periodic Motor Vehicle Inspection: A Comparative Data Analysis*, 1971.

Tie-In Sales. If the model of supplier (inspection stations) behavior is based on tie-in sales, a kind of behavior different from "nonprice" competition is assumed—one that restricts consumer choice. Given that vehicles must be certified if they are to be driven and that there is a relatively high fixed cost of inspection (time necessary to obtain the inspection plus the fixed inspection fee, whether or not the vehicle is approved), the demand for parts and repair service is not likely to be particularly responsive to changes in the prices charged for repairs. Hence, service stations offering inspection may charge higher prices, and perhaps require more repairs, than they would without required periodic inspections—if the inspection stations are the service stations that do the repairs. While all states allow the owner to have the repairs made elsewhere, they are most often made by the stations detecting the defect since drivers are inclined to minimize the time costs involved in obtaining a repair.

This tie-in sales behavior by suppliers would be more profitable in some settings than in others. For example, the practice of visibly labeling vehicles that fail inspection would alert all repair stations that the customer's demand elasticity for repairs is very low, that is, that the customer needs the repairs to be performed immediately and will pay a higher price than otherwise. Similarly, the demand for repairs should depend in part on how close the current inspection sticker is to expiration. The shorter the period of time until expiration, the less important the price of repairs should be, since there would be a reduced opportunity to locate an alternative source of repairs. Moreover, many vehicle owners wait until very close to the expiration date, making the opportunity cost of "balking" (that is, refusing to agree to the repairs required by a given inspector for approval) higher than it would be otherwise. This effect would seem to be magnified in those states which do not perform inspections year round (see Table 1). In effect, customers would be trading off a lower time cost of inspections for a higher pecuniary payment.

There is some evidence to support the "tie-in sales" hypothesis for suppliers' behavior. In a recent study issued by the Department of Transportation it was estimated that safety repair costs attributable to mandatory inspection requirements range from $30 to $90 per vehicle per year, depending on the age and type of vehicle and the stringency of inspection.[9] These estimates would suggest that periodic inspection requirements account for roughly 12 to 40 percent of average yearly vehicle maintenance and repair bills.[10] The experiment

[9] NHTSA, *Costs and Benefits of Motor Vehicle Inspection*, p. 14.
[10] Ibid., p. 13.

conducted in Pennsylvania noted earlier showed the estimated repair bill quoted by licensed inspection stations to be, on average, $22.67 higher than the estimated repair bill quoted by three independent stations for identical repairs.[11] In addition, the Pennsylvania study found that the "average estimated cost of repairs for nonexistent defects was $34.93."[12] These findings correspond quite closely to the range of additional expenditures reported by DOT.

Public Ownership and Inspection Provision

The empirical evidence presented above suggests that in those cases where periodic inspections were provided by state-owned and operated stations, there was no statistically significant net effect on accident rates. Presumably, publicly owned and operated stations would have little or no incentive to require repairs not needed, and also presumably these stations would be more attentive to mechanical problems than stations specializing in "minimum hassle" inspection service. In support of this theory, evidence from this study indicates that publicly owned and operated systems seem to have no effect on accident rates whereas private systems tend to be associated with higher death rates. This evidence is consistent with the hypothesis that, if drivers adjusted their behavior toward more risk-taking because they think inspection improves the condition of the cars, and it does not, the net effect of periodic inspection is to increase death rates; but if public provision of periodic inspection does improve the mechanical condition of the automobiles inspected, this improvement is merely canceled out by drivers' behavioral adjustments. But it is important to bear in mind that even a nonprofit structure for periodic inspection does not appear to offer net improvements in highway safety, though at least it does not make things worse (ignoring, of course, the cost of the inspection program).

Random Inspection Systems: An Underrated Alternative?

The findings here suggest that random or spot-check inspection procedures tend to reduce highway death rates or at least are accompanied by rates lower than those in nonrandom inspection states. While the statistical significance of this result is not sufficient to

---

[11] School of Urban and Public Affairs, *An Assessment of Pennsylvania's Periodic Motor Vehicle Inspection System*, p. 14. It should be stressed that the Pennsylvania inspection program is generally regarded as one of the best in existence.
[12] Ibid., p. 12.

provide definitive support for random inspection, the results do suggest that such programs may be more effective than periodic inspection. In any case, it implies that *NHTSA would be justified in allowing random inspection to be substituted for periodic inspection*, which it has not done on a permanent basis—on the grounds that it lacked evidence to show that random inspections were *as effective* as periodic inspection. That evidence is now available.

6

Regulation for Public or Special Interest

The first purpose of the empirical studies is to identify the purpose of the legislation! The announced goals of a policy are sometimes unrelated or perversely related to its actual effects, and the truly intended effects should be deducted from the actual effects.[1]

Attempts to explain the existence of vehicle inspection according to the view that it furthers the public interest are shaken by the fact that it does not seem to improve highway safety. This disparity between the stated objectives of periodic inspection and its actual performance will not surprise those economists and other observers who have become increasingly disenchanted with the view that regulation is designed and able to eliminate market failures. Their disenchantment has led to fundamental shifts in emphasis in currently propounded theories of regulation. Perhaps the most widely adopted alternative thesis (among economists, at least) is the view that regulation is designed and operated primarily for the benefit of the industry regulated.[2] This thesis—the "special interest" theory—has proven to have considerable predictive power in a number of cases, though most of

---

[1] George J. Stigler, "Supplementary Note on Economic Theories of Regulation (1975)," in George J. Stigler, *The Citizen and the State: Essays on Regulation* (Chicago: University of Chicago Press, 1975), p. 140.

[2] The "interest group" approach to regulation has emerged, by and large, from two seminal papers by Professor Stigler. George J. Stigler and Claire Friedland, "What Can Regulators Regulate? The Case of Electricity," *Journal of Law and Economics*, vol. 5 (October 1962); and George J. Stigler, "The Theory of Economic Regulation," *The Bell Journal of Economics and Management Science*, vol. 3 (Spring 1971), pp. 3-21. For examples of later developments and extensions, see Richard Posner, "Theories of Economic Regulation," *The Bell Journal of Economics and Management Science*, vol. 5, no. 2 (Autumn 1974), pp. 335-358; Sam Peltzman, "Toward a More General Theory of Regulation," *Journal of Law and Economics*, vol. 19, no. 2 (August 1976), pp. 211-240; and Richard Posner, "The Social Costs of Monopoly and Regulation," *Journal of Political Economy*, vol. 83, no. 4 (August 1975), pp. 807-827.

these involve traditional economic regulation rather than social or consumer protection regulation. For example, there is puzzlement over how the automobile industry benefits from safety-design legislation, the subject investigated by Peltzman.[3] While the stated purpose of periodic inspection is clearly social, its effects may more appropriately fall under the economic rubric.

The task of the present chapter is to investigate the applicability of the special interest theory of regulation to periodic vehicle inspection. Even though periodic inspection regulations may be ineffective in improving highway safety, they may have other effects and may serve other constituencies.

Mandatory periodic inspections result in large expenditures by vehicle owners. The burden of these expenditures is, however, distributed over a large and diverse group and is not likely to generate organized opposition. Even if this "taxed" group saw part of the inspection cost as a pure income transfer to station owners, organized opposition is not likely to arise because the per-driver cost of organizing an effective campaign to repeal inspection laws is greater than the potential per-driver benefits of such a move.[4] This is not to say that all the "tax" imposed on vehicle owners by periodic inspection requirements is a subsidy or net gain to groups or industries involved in providing inspections. Some of the costs are nonpecuniary (the time costs, for example) and therefore involve deadweight losses. Moreover, those industries that receive income transfers as a result of inspection laws may not end up with a profit, inasmuch as they must bear the costs of obtaining or protecting such transfers. These costs (for example, the cost of acquiring certification to be an official inspection station) seem likely to eliminate any long-run gains. Indeed,

---

[3] See the discussion in Henry L. Manne and Roger LeRoy Miller, *Auto Safety Regulation: The Cure or the Problem* (New Jersey: Thomas Horton and Daughters, 1976). At least two arguments have been made in this context. William Niskanen, p. 15, suggests the following:

> Assume a Congressman's special capacity is to be a broker for special favors. He either is a broker for getting money out of the government or getting favorable regulatory treatment, but one way or the other, out of the government. But he finds a peculiar industry that has never asked for any special favors, mostly because it figured out a way to run its cartel without government help. Under those circumstances, a Congressman has an incentive to create special costs, the relief of which then becomes a special favor.

Richard Posner, "Theories of Economic Regulation," p. 348, suggests a somewhat different explanation for the consistency of safety-design requirements with "private interest" regulation: "conceivably safety and emission controls hurt foreign manufacturers more than domestic ones."

[4] Opposition is also unlikely because many vehicle operators believe that inspections have a positive effect on driving safety. See Sherman, "Sampling of Driver Opinions."

they seem likely to produce a net welfare loss, since they will generally have no socially valuable by-products.

It is thus of interest to examine the expenditures and transfers involved in periodic inspection programs to see how various interests and sectors of the economy are affected by them.

Extent of the Transfers to Certified Inspection Agents

The gross receipts by certified inspection stations resulting from periodic inspection requirements are difficult to measure, since some expenditures obviously would be made on vehicle maintenance even in the absence of inspections. A rough estimate of the additional revenue gained by certified inspection stations can be obtained by examining the percentage of vehicles inspected in which no defects are found. This approximation is rough, for at least two reasons. First, as noted in Chapter 4, stations often find nonexistent defects thus reducing the percentage of vehicles which should have passed inspection and producing an underestimation of the revenue to station owners. Second, some of the vehicles that pass inspection without repairs or adjustments will have had repairs made in preparation for the inspection, producing an overstatement of the revenue.

In South Carolina, in 1976, some 78 percent of the vehicles inspected passed without any repairs or adjustments.[5] Applying this percentage to the country as a whole, Table 10 offers a tentative estimate of the gross transfer of resources to certified inspection stations in the various states. This tentative estimate represents 78 percent of the product of the net charge per inspection going to inspection stations and the number of registered vehicles in a state. The estimated gross transfer includes 78 percent of the stations' revenue from inspections (assuming roughly that those cars failing inspection would have been inspected even in the absence of periodic requirements). A more accurate calculation could be made, of course, if state-by-state data on the rate of passage without repairs were available. But, Table 10 indicates the general order of magnitude involved in the transfers. The estimates of the total annual additional expenditure by vehicle owners resulting from required periodic inspection—excluding repair and time costs—total nearly $200 million.

The extent to which this $200 million constitutes a subsidy to station operators depends, of course, on the costs of obtaining inspec-

[5] South Carolina State Highway Department, Motor Vehicle Division, *Annual Report, 1976-1977: Motor Vehicle Inspection.*

TABLE 10
Estimated Annual Transfers
to Certified Inspection Stations, 1976

State	Charge per Inspection (dollars)	Amount Going to State per Inspection (dollars)	Number of Registered Vehicles (thousands)	Gross Transfers (thousands of dollars)[a]
Arkansas	3.25	1.25	887	1,384
Colorado[b]	5.50 maximum	.10	1,490	12,552
Dist. of Columbia	3.00	0	245	573
Florida	3.00	.40	4,653	9,436
Georgia	3.00	.25	2,535	5,438
Hawaii[b]	4.50 maximum	1.50	412	1,919
Indiana	2.50–4.00	.50	2,597	4,558
Iowa	8.00	.25	1,573	9,509
Kentucky	2.00	.25	1,740	2,375
Louisiana	1.00	.25	1,731	1,013
Maine[b]	2.00	.20	524	1,471
Massachusetts[b]	2.00	0	2,844	8,873
Mississippi	2.50	.50	1,022	1,594
Missouri	3.50	.50	2,220	5,195
Nebraska	3.75	.40	848	2,216
New Hampshire[b]	5.00 average	.65	418	2,837
New Jersey	2.50[c]	.50[c]	3,882	6,056
New Mexico[b]	1.00	.10	579	813
New York	3.00	.25	6,867	14,730
North Carolina	3.10	.35	2,959	6,347
Oklahoma	2.00	.50	1,456	1,704
Pennsylvania[b]	4.00–8.00	.50	6,852	58,790
Rhode Island	4.00	1.00	508	1,189
South Carolina	3.00	.50	1,479	2,884
South Dakota	4.00	.25	345	1,009
Texas	4.00	1.00	6,357	14,875
Utah	5.25 maximum	.25	605	2,360
Vermont[b]	3.00 average	0	239	1,119
Virginia[b]	4.00	0	2,830	17,659
West Virginia	4.50	.50	759	2,368
Wyoming	2.00	.25	211	288
Total				197,308

[a] Based on 78 percent figure.

[b] Twice-yearly inspections.

[c] Indicates fee for reinspection only.

Sources: Correspondence with state administrative agencies; Motor Vehicle Manufacturers Association, *Motor Vehicle Facts and Figures 1977* (Detroit, 1977); American Association of Motor Vehicle Administrators, *Periodic Motor Vehicle Inspection: A Comparative Data Analysis, 1971* (Washington, D.C.).

tion certificates and providing inspection services. These costs vary according to such factors as local wage rates, the costs of specialized equipment necessary for inspections, and the costs of obtaining an inspection license. Expenditures on these factors would have to be netted out to determine the extent to which inspection agents gain from mandatory periodic inspection regulations.

Certification Fee Systems

In most states with periodic inspection, one of the costs to the inspection stations is the license or certification fee. Payment of the fee provides information on the locations, parties, and scale of the regulated activity (as well as, in some cases, being used to finance the activities of the regulatory authority).[6] Table 11 lists the fees required of stations seeking inspection certification in the various states, the state funds to which these fees are deposited, and the states where the fees (including sticker fees) are sufficient to pay for the state's costs in the inspection program.

Several observations may be made in connection with Table 11. First, since the certification fees in many states are earmarked for administering the program, these "tax" revenues from inspection agents are, in fact, being used for their benefit (the fees support the program that benefits the agents). Second, in roughly two-thirds of the inspecting states, the fees required of the inspecting agents fully support the inspection programs. One suspects this could lead to important mutual backscratching between inspection stations and those who monitor them. Third, earmarking funds for specific regulatory projects generally helps ensure the permanency of the projects, since the regulation (in this case, the mandatory periodic inspection program) is not dependent on the budgeting process and annual legislative review.[7]

Licensing and Entry Conditions

The special interest theory of regulation stresses that members of an interest group will typically seek resource transfers indirectly (for example, in the form of output limitations), rather than through

---

[6] See George J. Stigler, "The Process of Economic Regulation," *Antitrust Bulletin*, vol. 17, no. 1 (Spring 1972).

[7] This aspect of earmarking tax funds is stressed in William Landes and Richard Posner, "An Independent Judiciary in the Interest-Group Perspective," *Journal of Law and Economics*, vol. 18, no. 3 (December 1975).

TABLE 11

Financing of State Inspection Programs

State	Fees for Station Certification (dollars)	Annual Renewal Fee (dollars)	State Funds to Which Fees are Deposited	Do Fees Support Entire Program?[b]
Arkansas	25.00	10.00	State Police Operations Fund	Yes
Colorado	0	[c]	Highway Users Fund	Yes
Delaware	State Owned	State Owned	General Fund–State of Delaware	Yes
Florida	0	0	General Revenue Fund	Yes
Georgia	10.00	10.00	General Fund	Yes
Hawaii	0	0	County General Fund	No
Idaho[a]	0	0	Motor Vehicle	Yes
Indiana	30.00	0	Vehicle Inspection Revolving Fund	Yes
Iowa	5.00	5.00	State General Fund	[c]
Kentucky	25.00	25.00	Trust and Agency (To Support Inspection Program)	Yes
Louisiana	10.00	10.00	Trust and Agency Account for Motor Vehicle Inspection	Yes
Maine	2.00	2.00	Highway Fund	No
Massachusetts	[c]	[c]	Highway Fund	Yes
Mississippi	10.00	10.00	General Operating Fund of Department of Public Safety	No
Missouri	10.00	10.00	State Highway Fund	No
Nebraska	5.00	5.00	Safety Inspection Cash Fund	Yes
New Hampshire	15.00	15.00	Highway Fund	Yes
New Jersey	10.00	10.00	State Treasury (Reinspection Fees— Motor Vehicle Inspection Fund)	No
New Mexico[a]	5.00	5.00	General Fund	No
New York	25.00	25.00	Department of Motor Vehicles Fund	No
North Carolina	0	0	Special Fund for Program Administration	Yes

TABLE 11 (continued)

State	Fees for Station Certification (dollars)	Annual Renewal Fee (dollars)	State Funds to Which Fees are Deposited	Do Fees Support Entire Program?[b]
Oklahoma	25.00	5.00	Department of Public Safety	Yes
Pennsylvania	0	0	Motor Fund	Yes
Rhode Island	25.00	[c]	State General Fund	No
South Carolina	10.00	10.00	General Highway Fund	Yes
South Dakota	10.00	2.50	General Fund	Yes
Texas	30.00	[c]	Motor Vehicle Inspection Fund	Yes
Utah	0	0	Highway Maintenance and Construction Fund	No
Vermont	0	0	None	[c]
Virginia	0	0	Financed Through General Highway Funding	[c]
West Virginia	0	0	Department of Public Safety	Yes
Wyoming[a]	25.00	[c]	Vehicle Inspection	Yes

[a] Recently repealed inspection laws.

[b] Including sticker fees received by state per inspection (see Table 10, column 3).

[c] Information not supplied in questionnaire.

SOURCES: Correspondence with state administrative agencies; Association of Motor Vehicle Administrators, *Periodic Vehicle Inspections: A Comparative Data Analysis.*

direct subsidies, if the entry of new firms in the industry over time would dissipate the per capita returns achieved through regulation.[8] But, if control over new entrants can be built into the regulation, direct subsidies are preferable.

Occupational licensing or certification requirements have long been a subject of controversy. On the one hand, it is argued that such requirements are necessary to protect consumers from unqualified (or fraudulent) practitioners. On the other hand, limiting the

---

[8] See Stigler, "The Theory of Economic Regulation," p. 4; James M. Buchanan and Gordon Tullock, "Polluters' Profits and Political Response: Direct Controls versus Taxes," *American Economic Review*, vol. 65, no. 1 (March 1975); and Jean-Luc Migue, "Controls versus Subsidies in the Economic Theory of Regulation," *Journal of Law and Economics*, vol. 20, no. 1 (April 1977), pp. 213-222.

TABLE 12

CERTIFICATION REQUIREMENTS FOR INSPECTORS AND INSPECTION STATIONS

State	Station Manager	Inspectors	Must Pass Written Exam	Must Pass Performance Exam	Is Training Required?	Are Inspectors Qualified Mechanics?	Are Certifications for a Specified Period?	Is Inspection Station Required to Post Bond?
Arkansas	yes	yes	yes	yes	yes	yes	no	no
Colorado	yes	yes	yes	yes	yes	no	no	no
Delaware	yes	yes	yes	yes	yes	no	yes	no
District of Columbia	yes	yes	yes	yes	yes	yes	no	a
Florida	yes	yes	yes	yes	yes	no	no	no
Georgia	yes	yes	yes	yes	yes	yes	yes	no
Hawaii	no	yes	yes	yes	yes	no	yes	no
Idaho	yes	no	no	yes	no	yes	no	no
Indiana	yes	yes	a	no	no	yes	no	yes
Kentucky	yes	yes	yes	yes	yes	yes	yes	no
Louisiana	a	yes	no	yes	yes	yes	yes	yes
Maine	a	yes	yes	a	yes	yes	yes	no
Massachusetts	a	yes	no	yes	yes	yes	no	no
Mississippi	no	yes	yes	yes	yes	yes	yes	yes
Missouri	yes	yes	yes	yes	yes	yes	yes	no
Nebraska	no	no	no	no	a	yes	yes	yes
New Hampshire	yes	yes	a	yes	no	yes	yes	a
New Jersey	a	a	yes	a	a	no	a	a
New Mexico	no	no	no	no	no	no	yes	yes

New York	ᵃ	yes	no	yes	ᵃ	yes	no
North Carolina	yes	yes	yes	yes	no	no	no
Oklahoma	yes	no	yes	yes	yes	no	no
Pennsylvania	no	no	yes	yes	no	no	no
Rhode Island	no	yes	no	yes	yes	no	no
South Carolina	no	yes	yes	yes	yes	yes	no
South Dakota	no	yes	yes	yes	yes	yes	yes
Texas	no	yes	yes	yes	yes	yes	yes
Utah	yes	yes	yes	yes	ᵃ	yes	ᵃ
Vermont	no	yes	no	no	yes	no	no
Virginia	no	yes	yes	yes	yes	no	no
West Virginia	yes	yes	yes	yes	ᵃ	no	ᵃ
Wyoming	yes	no	no	no	no	no	yes

ᵃ No response provided in questionnaire.

SOURCE: Association of Motor Vehicle Administrators, *Periodic Vehicle Inspections: A Comparative Data Analysis.*

TABLE 13

Applications and Approvals for Inspection Station Certification, 1974–1976

State	1974			1975			1976		
	Number of applications	Number approved	Percent denied	Number of applications	Number approved	Percent denied	Number of applications	Number approved	Percent denied
Florida	d	d	d	81	41	49.0	104	57	45.0
Georgia	d	673	d	d	395	d	d	263	d
Iowa	d	d	d	d	d	d	1,000[a]	300[a]	70.0[a]
Kentucky	d	d	d	d	d	d	3,100[a]	d	0.3[a]
Louisiana	243	243	0[b]	227	227	0[b]	137	137	0[b]
Missouri	633	633	0[b]	966	966	0[b]	875	875	0[b]
Nebraska	d	126	d	223	178	20.0	203	159	22.0
New Jersey[c]	4,000[a]	3,500[a]	13.0	900[a]	1,294[a]	c	550[a]	486[a]	12.0
New York	d	d	d	2,157	2,074	4.0[b]	2,275	2,185	4.0[b]

North Carolina	769	d	3.0[a]	741	d	3.0[a]	931	d	3.0[a]
Oklahoma	492	491	0.2	336	331	2.0	431	431	0
Pennsylvania	2,522	2,069	18.0	3,516	2,171	38.0	3,997	2,251	44.0
South Carolina	303	226	25.0	433	330	24.0	527	420	20.0
Texas	1,151	1,116	3.0	1,152	1,142	0.9	1,156	1,136	2.0
Utah	245	224	9.0	297	260	13.0	266	235	12.0
Vermont	81	75	7.0	141	122	14.0	176	153	13.0
Virginia	d	216	50.0[a]	d	216	50.0[a]	d	202	50.0[a]
West Virginia	d	d	d	d	d	d	120	80	33.0

[a] Approximated by agency authorizing certifications.

[b] Stations are visited by field personnel prior to submitting the applications. Application accepted and submitted when the station is qualified for licensing.

[c] Reinspection stations—information reflects period from July 1975 through late 1977, hence there is some overlapping of applications and approvals.

[d] No response or information not available.

SOURCE: Correspondence with state administrative agencies.

number of competitors in an industry by licensure increases the average return to existing firms.[9] Requirements for obtaining inspection certification differ from state to state, though most would raise the costs of (or generally hinder) new entrants. Table 12 provides a breakdown on aspects of inspection certification likely to affect the costs of obtaining certification.

In addition to those limitations noted in Table 12, virtually all states have established minimum age and residency requirements. They generally require the inspection station to be open (with a qualified inspector on duty) for eight hours daily. Many states require that stations must have been in operation for a specified period of time, usually between six months to a year, before they can be granted certification. Another general requirement for certification involves the minimum dimensions of the inspection facility, ostensibly imposed because a certain distance is necessary to check head lights. But the wide variations in the required minimum dimensions suggest that this is not the sole question at issue.[10]

Apart from these specific requirements, certification is generally limited to persons of "good" character with a reputation for "sound business ethics" and "integrity." The laws fail to define such terms, so that interpretation is left to the discretion of the administration agencies. Table 13 shows the number of applications and approvals for inspection certification for several states for the years 1974 through 1976. Reasons most commonly given for denying an application include: improper facilities or lack of space, inadequate equipment, premises not in clean and orderly condition, improper facility location (two states), insufficient personnel, inability to meet business

---

[9] For an early and extensive economic analysis of the effects of occupational licensing, see Thomas G. Moore, "The Purpose of Licensing," *Journal of Law and Economics*, vol. 4 (October 1961). See also discussion of licensing and empirical analysis in Stigler, "The Theory of Economic Regulation," p. 13-17.

[10] Within the state of New York, for example, the minimum size specifications vary according to population density:

(i) Class 1 station: In a city or village having a population of less than 10,000 and in an area outside a city or village, in any county of the state, a minimum enclosed area of 300 square feet is required.

(ii) Class 2 station: In a city or village with a population of 10,000 or more, but less than 100,000 and in the county of Richmond, a minimum enclosed area of 600 square feet is required.

(iii) Class 3 station: In a city with a population of 100,000 or more, and in the counties of Bronx, New York, Kings, and Queens, a minimum enclosed area of 750 square feet is required.

State of New York Department of Motor Vehicles, *Regulations Affecting Inspection Section License Applicants* (Albany, New York: Bureau of Automotive Safety Standards, May 1975), p. 2.

hours requirements, licenses originally revoked, and previous complaints of improper or inadequate inspection.[11]

It should be reiterated that the net effect of standards for certifying inspectors and inspection stations—even though the standards make entry more costly—would be more difficult to evaluate if at the same time highway safety were improved. But with no evidence for improved highway safety, the unavoidable inference is that the standards, which raise the costs of obtaining certification, reduce the number of competing inspection stations, thus protecting the subsidies to existing firms. Table 14 shows the state-by-state average transfer per station for 1976 (using the estimates from Table 10).

These estimates range from an annual return of $7,413 in Florida to an annual return of $443 in Wyoming. The two states that repealed their mandatory inspection laws in 1977, New Mexico and Wyoming, had the lowest estimated receipts per station. Their repeal of periodic inspection laws is consistent with the special interest interpretation of this regulation; that is, it would be in those states with the lowest average gain per member of the relevant interest group, that the weakest support for mandatory inspection (and the weakest resistence to its repeal) would be expected.

The estimates provided in Table 14 suggest that certification requirements for inspection stations differ from state to state in their effectiveness as entry barriers. Where such barriers are ineffective, entry of new firms generally can be expected until the gains from obtaining inspection certification are driven to "normal" economic levels—that is, until there are no monopoly profits. In these states, even though the total expenditure for inspection fees may be large, an individual inspection station will not make an extraordinary profit from the periodic inspection requirement after equilibrium is reached. This does not imply, of course, that stations already certified would not support mandatory periodic inspection, since they will continue to earn more than normal profits during the period when new stations are being certified until, finally, monopoly profits disappear.

In those states where requirements are sufficient to restrict the entry of new stations, certified stations still may not earn above-normal profits in long-run equilibrium. Competition to protect existing certificates would still require an expenditure of resources that could eliminate the gains from holding a license. Under this type of "entry-barrier" setting, the potential gains from acquiring an inspection license would be predictably dissipated because of the competitive rivalry among stations to obtain a license. Thus, even if entry

---

[11] Author's correspondence with state agencies.

TABLE 14

AVERAGE RECEIPT PER CERTIFIED INSPECTION STATION

State	Number of Certified Inspection Stations	Ratio of Registered Vehicles to Number of Inspection Stations	Average Transfer per Station[a]
Arkansas	1,500	591.3	922.5
Colorado	3,500[b]	425.7	3,586.2
Delaware	NA	NA	NA
Florida	1,273	3,655.1	7,412.6
Georgia	2,900	874.1	1,875.0
Hawaii	630	650.7	3,045.7
Indiana	5,832	445.3	781.5
Iowa	1,900	827.9	5,004.6
Kentucky	3,300	527.3	719.7
Louisiana	1,652	1,047.8	612.9
Maine	1,700	308.2	865.5
Massachusetts	3,180[b]	894.3	2,790.3
Mississippi	1,379	741.1	1,156.1
Missouri	4,731	469.2	1,098.0
Nebraska	2,032	417.3	1,090.5
New Hampshire	1,762	237.2	1,609.8
New Jersey	4,600[c]	843.9	1,316.5
New Mexico	1,365[d]	424.1	595.5
New York	13,500	508.7	1,091.1
North Carolina	6,565	450.8	966.9
Oklahoma	2,214	657.6	769.4
Pennsylvania	17,841	384.1	3,295.2
Rhode Island	1,000	508.0	1,188.7
South Carolina	3,139	471.2	918.8
South Dakota	808[b]	426.9	1,248.9
Texas	7,300	870.8	2,037.7
Utah	1,755[b]	344.7	1,344.4
Vermont	1,075	222.3	1,040.4
Virginia	3,019	937.4	5,849.3
West Virginia	1,600	474.4	1,480.1
Wyoming	650[d]	324.6	443.1

[a] Based on expenditures estimated in Table 10.

[b] Number of Certified Inspection Stations in 1971 (all other figures reflect 1976 data).

[c] Reinspection stations.

[d] Inspection laws repealed in 1977.

SOURCES: Correspondence with state administrative agencies; Motor Vehicle Manufacturers Association, *Motor Vehicle Facts and Figures 1977;* Association of Motor Vehicle Administrators.

is restricted, the net result will be that inspection stations would not earn rents in long-run equilibrium because of the necessary expenditures or "rent-seeking" activity involved in obtaining and retaining licenses.[12] Even so, inspection stations in states where entry is effectively controlled would not be indifferent to inspection regulations. If it costs money for stations to obtain an inspection license, present license holders would suffer capital losses if mandatory inspection were ended. For example, suppose that in order to obtain an inspection license, a station has been constructed to the required dimensions and certain specialized equipment is purchased. Elimination of the inspection program would mean that the costs of special construction or special equipment would not be offset by revenues from inspection. Obviously such stations would therefore suffer losses.

In sum, periodic inspection laws tend to increase the transfers to certified inspection agents because vehicle owners must pay inspection fees and incur additional repair bills. There may not, however, be net gains to inspection stations even with attempts to restrict entry through licensing procedures. This does not mean that certified inspection stations generally would not support periodic inspection requirements. Quasi-rents may be earned during the transition from no system to a system of inspections, and losses would predictably result during a subsequent transition if the program were terminated.

Effects of Inspection Laws on Vehicle-Related Industries

An additional sector of the economy likely to be affected by inspection regulations includes those industries involved in manufacturing replacement parts and accessories or providing automotive repair services. Mandatory inspections obviously affect the demand for the products and services supplied by these industries (as noted in Chapter 5 in connection with tie-in sales). The figures presented in Chapter 5 suggest that mandatory inspection and required repair or replacement of parts increase maintenance expenditures (that is, in technical terms, there is reduction in the elasticity of demand for repair service and parts replacement). If, as these estimates suggest, additional expenditures on vehicle maintenance in periodic inspection states may run as high as 12 to 40 percent above those in noninspection states, then for the 76 million vehicles inspected in 1976, additional expenditures

---

[12] For analyses and empirical estimates of welfare losses due to rent-seeking activity see Gordon Tullock, "The Welfare Cost of Tariffs, Monopolies, and Theft," *Western Economic Journal*, vol. 5, no. 3 (June 1967), pp. 224-232; Anne O. Krueger, "The Political Economy of the Rent-Seeking Society," *American Economic Review*, vol. 64, no. 2 (June 1974), pp. 291-303; and Posner, "The Social Costs of Monopoly and Regulation."

would range roughly from $2 to $7 billion. The cost of repairs (because of price inelasticity or unneeded repairs) is substantially greater than the fixed inspection fees.

Note that transfers of income of this sort imply that inspection regulations weigh most heavily on the poor, since the poor typically have older cars. In other words, the income redistribution is regressive.

Of course, all the transfer of resources from vehicle owners to the parts and repair service industries may not be a pure subsidy: owners presumably get something in return for their additional expenditures (fewer breakdowns, longer average life of vehicles, even if not reduced accidents). There is some evidence to suggest that mandatory periodic inspections do tend to increase the average service life of vehicles, which, presumably, has an adverse economic effect on automobile manufacturers.[13] Since most of these firms also manufacture replacement parts and accessories, the net effect of inspection laws on the industry is not clear.

Deadweight Welfare Losses

All the effects of inspection regulations cannot be considered as transfers or redistributions of income, since welfare losses occur when the benefit from an expenditure of resources is not as high as the benefit from this expenditure put to alternative use, a point particularly important with respect to the time spent in taking a car through inspection. If, as is usually done in such analysis, the value of the owner's time is estimated at his wage rate, this loss can be significant. For example, if time is valued at the 1976 average wage of about $8.00 per hour and if an inspection took, say, thirty minutes (including the time driving to and from the inspection station), the time cost would be $4.00, which is greater than the fee charged for inspections in most states. The time costs imposed on vehicle owners do not represent transfers or gains to anyone and, hence, are pure welfare losses. Given that some 76 million vehicles were inspected in 1976, this welfare loss is probably in excess of $300 million annually.

---

[13] Several studies report a causation between compulsory periodic inspecting and longer vehicle life. For examples, see Alex Pellijeff, *Periodic Inspection of Motor Vehicles in Sweden: Organization and Statistics* (Sweden: Svensk Bilporvning); and Tony Hogg in *Road and Track*, vol. 28, no. 2 (October 1976), p. 31. It is noteworthy that in cost-benefit evaluations of inspection programs, induced vehicle longevity typically has been considered a benefit. See NHTSA, *Costs and Benefits of Motor Vehicle Inspection*, p. 12. But this is not necessarily true, since individual motor vehicle owners presumably can make efficient depreciation decisions according to their own internal (subjective) discount rates. Hence, longer vehicle service life might not be a net benefit of mandatory inspection programs.

There is an additional welfare cost of inspection regulations if stations expend resources in the competition to obtain inspection licenses. As discussed above, when there are potential above-normal profits (that is, economic rents) from holding a license, stations are willing to incur costs in seeking to obtain a license. Expenditure of resources devoted to such "rent-seeking" activity reduces the aggregate welfare of society since these resources could be used in alternative ways of greater value to society. The welfare loss from such rent-seeking activity caused by mandatory inspection could possibly approach $200 million annually (the amount of the additional revenues received from inspection). Moreover, this $200 million does not include revenues from additional sales of parts and service, and the estimate is most probably too low.

Two Observations

In general, the correspondence between the stated objectives of inspection programs and their actual effects is sufficiently weak to suggest alternative hypotheses for explaining mandatory periodic inspection. The theory of economic regulation which stresses the gains to special interests offers useful insights here, a point of particular interest because the theory has been developed primarily in the analysis of economic regulation and has not been applied to social regulation (including consumer-protection regulation). This special interest approach would predict that the primary proponents of a nationally standardized inspection program are those trade associations of industries involved either directly in providing inspections or indirectly in manufacturing and distributing vehicle parts and accessories.[14]

The stated goals of a nationally coordinated inspection program and the goals of many of the existing state systems are being broadened to encompass the control of automobile emissions and gasoline consumption through mandatory periodic tune-ups. The present study does not address the efficiency of inspection programs in accomplishing these additional objectives. It does suggest that these additional objectives be justified on their own merits and not simply on the grounds that they represent only a small additional cost to the existing regulatory apparatus—since that program, itself, has not been justified. To say the least, it is ironic that a program with no demonstrated effectiveness is being expanded to encompass additional aspects of motor vehicle operation.

---

14 In fact, this does turn out to be the case. See, for example, the study sponsored by several trade associations cited in note 4, Chapter 1.

7
Summary and Conclusion

In 1967, following the mandate of Congress, the U.S. Department of Transportation issued guidelines saying that states must implement periodic motor vehicle inspection programs or risk the cut-off of sizable federal aid. The stated objective of this federal initiative was to improve highway safety. In view of the resultant widespread implementation of vehicle inspection programs, the enormous costs associated with them, recent moves to expand their scope to include energy and environmental checks, and the overall importance of highway safety, it seems appropriate to ask whether these programs have been effective.

As of 1974 (the latest year for which requisite data are available) not all states had adopted vehicle inspection programs and there was considerable variation among those that had complied, with respect to the frequency of inspection, universal versus random checks, public versus private stations, and other aspects. Taking into account the major factors that would be expected to have an effect on highway safety, statistical techniques were employed in this study to determine the efficacy of vehicle inspection programs.

The basic hypothesis of this study is that, everything else being equal, accident rates will be significantly lower in states having vehicle inspection programs. However, the statistical tests revealed the strong conclusion that vehicle inspection programs have no detectable impact on highway safety. This conclusion is valid whether inspections are required once or twice yearly and whether the inspection stations are publicly or privately operated. Various plausible explanations are offered for this failure of vehicle inspection programs to fulfill their intended purpose.

A second important finding is that random inspection programs are at least as effective as periodic inspection programs and perhaps even more effective. This finding argues that the National Highway Traffic Safety Administration should use its statutory discretion to permit random inspection programs to be substituted for periodic inspections on a permanent basis. From the motorists' standpoint, random inspection systems are clearly preferable because they are less costly. This is not to imply that random inspection systems are cost-effective in reducing highway accidents. In fact, neither type of inspection program seems to have done the job. But of the two types, random inspection systems are clearly preferable because they are less cost.

While periodic inspection is merely ineffective in reducing accidents, other effects are not as innocuous. Vehicle inspection programs require large expenditures by vehicle owners. At least some of this expenditure represents transfers and potential gains to various groups or industries involved in the provision of inspections, replacement parts, and repair services. Although the competition to obtain these transfers ("rent-seeking" competition) may eliminate any net gains in the long run, there still appear to be incentives for various special interest groups to favor mandatory periodic inspection and an expansion of the requirements. The recent efforts of numerous trade associations involved in inspection-related activities to establish even more stringent criteria with an expanded scope that would include emission control and mandatory tune-ups and to transfer administrative responsibility to the federal government are evidence of this effect.

These findings have broader relevance for public policy. In general, they warn against the implementation of a costly nationwide program without good information on its likely effects. In this case the raw data were available—many state programs were already in place—but little or no attempt was made to use this information. This episode also shows the difficulty of redirecting or even terminating an inefficient program once in place—especially one in the sensitive area of public safety. Despite admission by NHTSA that little evidence exists to justify the program, congressional support for it continues unabated, and one hears increasing calls for the program to be expanded.

Periodic inspection may not—apparently does not—benefit the public, but it clearly benefits the special interest groups. Like Charles Dickens's Pip, periodic inspection requirements may have been sparked by great expectations. And like those of Pip (in the original version), the expectations have only a nodding acquaintance with reality.

APPENDIX A

Alternative Specifications of the Empirical Model

The regression results discussed in Chapter 4 are highly representative of findings from alternative specifications of the model which included different sets of control variables. In none of some 200 alternative equations examined was there any indication that periodic inspection programs have a positive effect in the sense of reducing highway death or accident rates. The versions included in the text were those with the best overall explanatory power, the most consistently significant coefficients on the independent variables, and the most stable across the different models.

An alternative worth mentioning is a specification that omits the minimum damage variable from the equations which examine the measures of nonfatal accident rates, because this variable never appears at statistically significant levels. Excluding this variable from the equations in the text makes virtually no difference in the significance levels or in the magnitude of the estimated coefficients presented in Tables 3 through 6. This variable was left in the equations since there is a clear a priori reason to suspect that it might account for some variations reported in nonfatal accident rates across states, even though, a posteriori, the empirical results suggest otherwise.

Finally, Table 15 presents the results of a model which includes the four inspection system binary variables in a single equation. A negative and significant sign on each respective variable would indicate that the particular system or aspect of a system is effective in reducing accident rates. The results portrayed in Table 15 suggest that periodic inspection systems—whether annual, biannual, or state-owned—are ineffective in producing highway safety improvement. The estimated coefficients for these three variables (periodic inspection, biannual inspection, and state-owned provisions) are not sta-

TABLE 15

COMBINED EFFECTS OF INSPECTION SYSTEMS

Independent Variable	Dependent Variables		
	Death rate	Nonfatal injury rate	Nonfatal accident rate
Constant	−0.86 (−0.34)	−2.84 (−0.78)	−4.06 (−1.16)
Periodic inspection	0.78 (0.90)	−0.04 (−0.28)	−0.07 (−0.56)
Biannual inspection	0.01 (0.13)	0.01 (0.05)	0.02 (0.18)
State-owned provision	0.18 (1.09)	−0.09 (−0.39)	−0.12 (−0.53)
Random inspection	−0.33 (−0.33)	−0.17 (−1.21)	−0.19 (−1.36)
Population density	−0.17 (−5.27)	0.10 (2.01)	0.10 (2.21)
Fuel consumption	0.08 (1.85)	−0.09 (−1.35)	−0.09 (−1.49)
Median income	−0.75 (−3.36)	1.50 (4.61)	1.54 (4.94)
Federal highways	0.02 (0.96)	0.06 (2.20)	0.04 (1.84)
Population age	−0.21 (−0.40)	−1.68 (−2.23)	−1.48 (−2.05)
License renewal	−0.06 (−0.89)	0.17 (1.71)	0.18 (1.91)
Alcohol consumption	0.09 (0.99)	−0.22 (−1.59)	−0.22 (−1.65)
Reporting minimum	—	−0.004 (−0.06)	0.01 (0.08)
R^2	0.7669	0.5567	0.5972
F (11,38)	11.36	3.87	4.57
N observed	50	50	50

tistically significant, and all three have the opposite sign from what might be expected. The estimated coefficient on the random inspection system variable is negative in all three equations and is significant at the 15 percent level in the two equations for nonfatal accident rates. Generally, the results presented in Table 15 lead to the same policy conclusions reached in the text, namely that there is no empirical support for the proposition that periodic inspection systems improve highway safety.

APPENDIX B

Test for Reverse Causation

The interpretation of the results reported in Chapter 4 are subject to question if, prior to the issuance of the NHTSA inspection standards, there were even greater differences in accident/fatality rates between subsequently adopting and nonadopting states than there were after the programs were put into effect. That is, adopting mandatory inspection procedures may have decreased accident/fatality rates but not below the levels experienced in noninspecting states with lower accident rates. In such circumstances, the cross-sectional regression analyses could fail to identify the true effects of vehicle inspection programs. To examine this issue in more detail, a cross-sectional model for 1965 was developed, and the results are compared with those for 1974.

Not all of the data on the variables employed in the 1974 model are available for 1965, mainly because NHTSA (responsible for much subsequent data collection) had not yet been established. A reasonable facsimile, however, was developed. The basic form of the 1965 model includes the following independent variables: (1) existence (and nature of) inspection systems in 1974, as defined in Chapter 4; (2) population density; (3) fuel consumption; (4) median family income; (5) federal highways; and (6) population age. The results of estimating this model (again using the logarithmic transformations of all continuous variables) are presented in Table 16. In order to economize in presenting these results, all four of the inspection system variables are included in a single equation, corresponding to the form of the model presented in Appendix A. T-ratios are listed in parentheses.

The 1965 results for fatal vehicle accidents suggest that reverse causation is not a problem with interpreting the 1974 estimates. In none of the four categories of inspection systems do we observe

TABLE 16
Highway Death Rates, 1965

Independent Variable	Dependent Variable
	Death rate
Constant	4.82
	(1.90)
Periodic inspection	−0.01
	(−0.85)
Biannual inspection	0.13
	(1.32)
State-owned inspection	−0.04
	(0.23)
Random inspection	−0.04
	(−0.41)
Population density	−0.05
	(−1.60)
Fuel consumption	0.40
	(1.58)
Median income	−0.58
	(−2.85)
Federal highways	0.11
	(0.26)
Population age	−0.01
	(−0.09)
$R^2 = 0.5250$	
$F_{(9,40)} = 4.91$	
N observed $= 50$	

statistically significant differences in the fatality rates in 1965 between states that had programs in operation in 1974 and states that did not. The R^2 is slightly lower than for the 1974 models, but this is to be expected because of the absence of some of the explanatory variables available for the latter year. In sum, there does not appear to be a reverse causation problem with the 1974 results, since the differentials in the death rates in inspecting versus noninspecting states were not diminished between 1965 and 1974.